Praise for

CW00506994

'A stunning book, exquisitel
with enormous compassioɪ
page of *Spring Tides* gives the reader everything they want:
poetry, knowledge, bejewelled specifics of the ocean and its
creatures. As we read, we grow richer, too. You will fall in
love with this book, treasure it, and keep it somewhere safe'
Monique Roffey, author of *The Mermaid of Black Conch*,
Costa Book of the Year 2020

'Insightful and brimming with marvels, this story of one
woman's love of an island opens a window to our entire
ocean, why it matters and how to protect it. At a time
when the rampant decline of nature can feel overwhelming, Gell offers a reasoned and much-needed ray of hope,
showing that it is possible to safeguard livelihoods and the
ocean's living treasures, and that it doesn't have to be a
choice between the two'
Helen Scales, author of *The Brilliant Abyss*
and *What a Shell Can Tell*

'It will appeal to the inner naturalist and to the child
within who scours rock pools, seeks treasure troves of
drifting shells, and marvels at a Maiden's Purse . . . Gell's
writing is as enticing as it is informative'
Lynn Buckle, *The Irish Times*

'Fiona Gell describes a life dedicated to the preservation
of a delicate habitat with a stirring, even spiritual, commitment'   *TLS*

'I loved *Spring Tides*. Seeding hope and wonder for future generations is a courageous calling and this is a beautifully-crafted triumph. The interweaving of motherhood with marine science, climate and the immeasurable pleasures of our own seashores is a pure delight. Please read this book!'
Nicholas Crane, author of *The Making of the British Landscape*

'Fiona Gell writes with the understanding of a scientist and the soul of a poet . . . Her descriptions are so vivid that as you read you can almost feel the lick of saltwater on your skin and smell the desiccating seaweed of a summer low tide'   Callum Roberts, author of *The Ocean of Life*

'A beautiful, briny portrait of one woman's infatuation with the sea. Fiona Gell has been steeped in salt water her whole life, and her deep understanding, knowledge of and love for her subject shines through'
Cal Flyn, author of *Islands of Abandonment*

'It's a rare treat to read a book about the sea that is as professional as it is passionate. Fiona Gell's experience and immersion in her subject is impressive'
Tristan Gooley, author of *The Natural Navigator*

'Anyone bound for the sea should be armed with this exceptional and engaging book'   *Country Life*

'A passionate, moving account of the transformative power of the sea'
Martin Chilton, *Independent* 'Book of the Month'

Dr Fiona Gell has a PhD in seagrass ecology and over twenty years' experience working in marine science, conservation and policy on small islands around the world. More recently she has worked on the Isle of Man's response to the climate emergency and has completed an MSc in climate change. She grew up on the Isle of Man and still lives there with her husband and son. She is also a published poet.

First published in Great Britain in 2022 by Weidenfeld & Nicolson,
This paperback edition first published in Great Britain in 2023
by Weidenfeld & Nicolson,
an imprint of The Orion Publishing Group Ltd
Carmelite House, 50 Victoria Embankment
London EC4Y 0DZ

An Hachette UK Company

1 3 5 7 9 10 8 6 4 2

A CIP catalogue record for this book is
available from the British Library.

ISBN (Mass Market Paperback) 978 1 4746 2186 1
ISBN (eBook) 978 1 4746 2187 8
ISBN (Audio) 978 1 4746 2188 5

Typeset by Input Data Services Ltd, Bridgwater, Somerset

Printed in Great Britain by Clays Ltd, Elcograf S.p.A.

www.weidenfeldandnicolson.co.uk
www.orionbooks.co.uk

Spring Tides

Exploring Marine Life of the Isle of Man

FIONA GELL

WEIDENFELD & NICOLSON

To Rob and Dylan

'The amen of calm waters,
The amen of calm waters,
The amen of calm waters.'

Derek Walcott, 'A Sea-Chantey',
In a Green Night, 1962

Contents

Prologue

This is my earliest memory. I am three years old and I sit in the bottom of my great-uncle's pot boat and take off the bands from the lobsters' claws. The deepest of blues, they creak over the bilges with robotic limbs towards my father's bare feet as he rows. Over the smell of the bait is the fresh, sweet scent of wrack on the shore.

This book has come from over twenty years of studying the sea and trying to protect it, and a lifetime of loving our other world beneath the waves. The sea is my work and my passion. I have been its advocate in situations where I must be reasoned, considered and evidence-based. But I am also seduced and obsessed by the infinite diversity of the sea, its breath-stopping beauty and capacity for surprise.

I have stood frozen in primitive fear as a basking shark, its granite skin dappled by sunlight, looms under the boat for long seconds. I have dived on our temperate horse mussel reefs, where the queen scallops are encrusted in golden sponges and the crimson squat lobsters wave their claws in the current, laughing with delight into my regulator. I have breathed deep on the bow of a scallop dredger in the twilight before dawn as we make our way to the fishing grounds, the crew on the deck smoking in silence as the sun begins to rise out of the dark, silver sea.

My energy comes from looking down into clear water through glossy kelp, studded with blue-rayed limpets, striped with iridescent blue; from swimming on my back at night making glowing wings of phosphorescence; from diving down into the magnetic blue beyond the reef; from drifting at speed past a carnival of coral in the company of mirrored jacks; from learning from a laughing fisherwoman how to find clams with my toes in the soft sand between the seagrass on a remote Indian Ocean shore.

Up until the birth of my son, eight years ago, I was a marine conservationist because I believed it was our responsibility to look after the planet and because of my personal connection to the sea. Now I am doing it for Dylan too. In Welsh his name means son of the sea or great tide and he is going to inherit the ocean I've studied and played a tiny part in trying to protect. He and his contemporaries are also going to inherit a rapidly and disastrously warming planet, a legacy to which I've also contributed and for which I want to make amends.

But there is hope. Through Dylan's enthusiasm and sheer delight in the marvels of our marine realm, I am rediscovering the love of the sea that first captivated me as a child. It is impossible to walk on the beach with him without seeing something new or gaining a fresh perspective on something I've started to take for granted. The bright orange beaks of oystercatchers as they fly towards the sea, the emerald blobs of green-leaf worm eggs tethered to sand like tiny balloons, the whorls and shards of shell in white and pink and orange and blue that rearrange themselves on every tide. Dylan's shock at pain or injustice has reignited my determination when it has become worn down. An unintentional glimpse of a photo of the Faroe Islands' whale cull on a news website, the horror of the sea turned red with blood and the incomprehension that people have chosen to do this. And closer to home, the housing estates rapidly encroaching on the saltmarsh nature reserve where we walk, the building debris caught in the brambles and flapping from the tops of the hawthorn trees. In the windows of houses in our town – 'Save our Bay' and Dylan's question every time we see them: 'Is it saved yet?' I hear myself saying, 'Well, it's not that simple', weighed down with the balance that comes from the third of my life spent as a civil servant. But you know, it *should* be simple. We should be able to save our bays and our reefs, our waters and our whales. This sounds like such an old refrain but today we need it more than ever and I'm writing in the hope that this is the decade in which we do save our seas. And Dylan's disbelief that humans could deliberately destroy their environment, and the rising voices of young people around the world calling for change, really does give me hope. I fervently hope that in Dylan's lifetime he will see a transformation in the way we take care of our lifegiving planet.

I believe that the tide has turned.

Exploring the sea in Port Erin, Isle of Man, aged four.

Spring Tides

If I crouch down low to peer at a citrus-coloured encrusting sponge at the furthest reaches of the spring tide, the largest tides of the month when the sea reaches highest up the beach at high tide, and retreats the furthest at low tide, the kelp stipes tower above me and I am transported. Not sea and not land, this is a netherworld of creaking holdfasts and the salt drip of a still-retreating tide. Though I've dived and snorkelled through submerged kelp forests and seen them as the ballan wrasse see them, I still delight in the enchantment that is the lowest of low tides. The long stretch of the kelp forest bends and bows and trails down the beach. Silhouetted against an evening sky it advances out of the ebbing mercury tide like an army of slick, long-haired warriors.

Spring tides can bring a sense of surprise, as if the sub-tidal world has been exposed unexpectedly before it could tidy itself away. It is the time when the rotund, jewel-hued buttons of cushion starfish can be found out in the open, not secreted under a rock, and when the fudge-coloured butterfish and sparkling dragonets are stranded in shallow pools, and gaze back still and astonished as you peer into their tidal retreats.

Low tide on Spaldrick beach, Port Erin, Isle of Man.

I know that I have been very privileged to have dived in the cool, clear waters of the Irish Sea and around the world, and to have spent more time than most among the fish. But the treat of a low spring tide is an experience open to many more people and one that, when I'm there, I always wish that I indulged in more regularly. When I have the chance to be on the seabed, among the holdfasts and sponges, but breathing weed-tanged air, my connection to the sea feels stronger than ever.

These glimpses give us hope, as we see the diversity of

life and the building blocks of a functioning ecosystem, a textbook food web at our fingertips. They give us joy, from spotting something we've never seen before; the purple frilled egg casts of a sea slug or the dazzling array of star ascidians, colonial sea squirts topped with childishly drawn flowers, like clusters of decorated cupcakes. The kelp itself is growing rapidly and converting carbon dioxide from our warming atmosphere to sugars which are stored in the kelp while it lives. When it dies and sinks to the deep seabed, the carbon can be locked away in the sea for aeons, helping us to reduce the impacts of climate change.

Down among the anemones, I am also reminded of the vulnerability of the ocean. Like the soft body of a hermit crab temporarily between shells, the sea is exposed to overfishing, habitat destruction, the invasive species we've spread around the globe and the accelerating impacts of warming seas.

But let's return to the hope. For decades, one of the biggest challenges with marine conservation and climate change has been the lack of visual prompts to act. Seeing a rainforest burn or a beloved place lost to development provides a clear cue that nudges us to action, but what has happened to our sea and our atmosphere has been largely invisible. Spring tides give us a unique opportunity to connect to the sea, to nature and to our mother planet. We can stand, firm footed, on a little piece of seabed that may only be uncovered a handful of times in a decade. Once we've made that connection we are committed, and life will never be the same again. A cerise cushion star, a goggle-eyed goby and a cup-cake ascidian – a rallying cry in miniature for us all to change the world.

I

Coming Home

'Then you may go the earth over and see grander things a thousand times, things more sublime, more beautiful; but you will come back to Manxland and tramp the Mull Hills, in May, long hour in and long hour out, and look at the flowering gorse and sniff its flavour; or lie by the chasms and listen to the screams of the sea-birds as they whirl and dip and dart and skim over the Sugar-loaf Rock, and you'll say, after all, that God has smiled on our little island, and that it is the fairest spot in His beautiful world.'

Hall Caine, *The Little Manx Nation*, 1891

It's October 2003 and I've just made a tentative contribution at a gathering of marine conservationists that's been met by an uncomfortable silence. There are about ten of us squashed into the front room of a terraced house in Douglas on the Isle of Man. Most of those present are volunteers supporting the marine work of an environmental charity and everyone is passionate about the sea. We're about a kilometre away from the Irish Sea, on a little island right in the middle of it. The Isle of Man is a

Crown dependency of the UK, like Jersey and Guernsey, so fiercely independent in many ways, with our own government and laws and our unique Celtic language and heritage. Yet constitutionally we are strongly linked to the UK, with the Queen presiding in the ancient capacity of Lord of Mann. Neatly equidistant between Britain and Ireland, we look in both directions.

Until my question about the group's plans to promote marine protected areas, I've not spoken throughout the meeting, except to smilingly acknowledge the warm welcome from my colleague who had invited me to join the group. An experienced diver with an amazing knowledge of the Isle of Man's marine life, he was the diving co-ordinator at Port Erin Marine Laboratory where I'd just started work.

There is a pause before someone gently breaks the silence to say that since things had gone so badly with the attempted Calf of Man designation over ten years ago, they had concentrated their efforts on other marine conservation projects and it wasn't something they were actively working on at the moment. Around me the other sea life enthusiasts shift uncomfortably and nod their heads in agreement, some of them looking apologetic.

I was a little stunned. I'd just spent four years researching marine protected areas (MPAs) around the world. Known variously as marine reserves, marine parks, marine conservation zones (and many other word combinations besides), these are areas of the sea protected from fishing, development and other impacts, which allow nature to thrive and replenish surrounding areas. I'd corresponded with leading scientists to put together a review of how protected areas can benefit fisheries and the marine environment. I'd given presentations at international conferences and published in leading scientific journals. I may not have admitted it then, but a dream of setting up MPAs around the Isle of Man was probably one of the reasons I'd been so keen to come back to the island where I'd grown up.

I knew that the attempt in the early 1990s to designate an islet off the south of the main island, the Calf of Man, as the Isle of Man's first Marine Nature Reserve (MNR) had been fraught with difficulty. I'd vaguely followed it as an undergraduate in the UK, hearing a little about it on my holidays back on the Isle of Man. But I'd had no idea about the scars it had left in the community. When I'd sailed back to Manx shores I was thirty years old, enthusiastic and almost evangelical about putting the theory I'd learnt into practice. I was also, inevitably, immersed in a very academic approach to marine conservation. I knew how to select the best habitat and how important it was to protect spawning areas and nursery areas. I knew (and had stated dozens of times in papers, articles and lectures) how important it is that you 'engage the community' and 'work with stakeholders', but I was only just beginning to understand what that really meant. I'd spent much of my PhD and post-doctoral research working with fishermen and fishing communities, going out on boats with them, learning about how they fished and interviewing them about the changes they'd seen and the challenges they lived with day to day. So, that's what was in my mind when I thought about stakeholder engagement. And while working with fishermen is one of the most important keys to marine conservation success, I still had a lot to learn. The attempted designation of the Calf had created division and dispute, between fishermen, community leaders and others who felt they had to defend their traditional practices and way of life, and scientists, divers and conservationists who wanted to protect the remarkable biodiversity and beauty of the Calf's marine life. It had become an example of how the most well-intentioned conservation plans can go awry and had left rifts between people. I wanted to use what I'd learnt about marine protected areas to make protecting the sea possible again.

It is hard to describe the enchantment of the Calf of Man. It is like a steep-sided chunk of the main island transplanted off the southern end, like an errant full stop. High cliffs surround it, and it is embraced by some of the strongest currents in Manx waters. It takes only about half an hour to get there by boat from Port Erin or Port St Mary but it feels like another world. It is often buffeted by strong winds, like the rest of the Isle of Man, but when it is calm the peace of the Island is almost palpable. The 250 hectares (less than two Hyde Parks or two and a half Sefton Parks) of the Calf somehow feel much larger than this. You can never really see the whole of the Island and it is criss-crossed with paths and sheep runs and for an occasional visitor it is possible to get disorientated, if not altogether lost.

This little island has a surprisingly colourful history. Calf is derived from its Viking name, *Kalfr*, meaning a small island near a larger one. It was thought to have been home to religious hermits as far back as the eighth century. A fragment of an early-medieval stone crucifix that was found in the ruins of a keill (a small chapel) there in the eighteenth century suggested its religious importance. The Calf of Man crucifixion altar slab, now on display in the Manx Museum in Douglas, is intricately carved in a swirling Byzantine style and could date back as far as those early hermits. The Calf was transferred between various owners over centuries and there were at least three attempts to introduce deer for hunting, none of which was ultimately successful. Rabbits abound though and it is grazed by loaghtan sheep, a tough, cliff-loving Manx breed of brown sheep with extravagantly curly horns.

One of the things for which the Calf was most notable over many centuries was its populations of seabirds. A Norse saga recounts how in 1014 a large party of Vikings (with over a hundred boats anchored off the Calf) was attacked by thousands of birds that in translation were called ravens. Two men were killed in the attack and the incident was recorded by the superstitious Vikings as a supernatural warning. It is now thought that those birds may have been Manx shearwaters which are thought to have been present in the tens of thousands historically. Manx shearwaters are found from the Arctic right down to the Antarctic and are largely considered an Atlantic bird. The size of the Calf colony is thought to have been the origin of the name Manx shearwater, but they were actually known first as the Manx puffin. They are small gull-like birds with a dark head and wings and pale underside. Like puffins, they nest on the ground in burrows and they migrate enormous distances. One Manx shearwater ringed on the Calf of Man was recorded again just fifty-one days later in São Paulo, Brazil.

In more recent times, the Calf has become best known as a bird observatory, with the only inhabitants often being bird wardens who stay for eight months of the year, leaving for the windiest, most desolate months of the winter. The wardens are now joined by volunteers and increasingly by tourists and staycationers, with the Calf being the only holiday option where you can leave the Island while remaining in Manx territory. It's not just birdwatchers that book the sparse accommodation at the Calf now. It has become popular for family holidays and has even been known to host an occasional, unusual hen night.

For a long time, the biggest immediate threat to ground nesting birds like Manx shearwaters was the Calf's once thriving population of brown rats, thought to have originally colonised from the wreck of a Russian ship in 1786. Rats inhabit a special place in Manx superstition. Some of the old Manx people thought that it was extremely bad luck to say the name of this common rodent and it has evolved numerous alternative names – long tail, ringie, R-A-T, queerfella and various responses to hearing the real name spoken, including whistling and knocking on wood. Before the arrival of rats on the Calf of Man, Manx shearwaters were reported to have thrived and the population was believed to have been the largest in the world at the time. An ambitious rodent elimination programme led by Manx National Heritage who own the Calf of Man started in 2012 and has successfully controlled rat populations and allowed the Manx shearwater to recover from a handful of nesting pairs to over 600 in recent years.

In 1990 the Isle of Man Government introduced the Wildlife Act, a significant piece of legislation which afforded legal protection to birds, marine mammals like grey seals and minke whale, turtles, basking sharks and the rare marine plant eelgrass. The Act also allowed the designation of Areas of Special Scientific Interest, National Nature Reserves and Marine Nature Reserves.

In 1990 I was seventeen and in sixth form in Ramsey in the north of the Island, taking A-levels in sciences and English literature and hoping to study biology at university. The long sandy sweep of Ramsey Bay was a backdrop to after-school chats with my friends at the end of the stone piers that mark the entrance to the harbour, and for the occasional night-time swims in the planktonic phosphorescence after the pub had closed. The previous year I'd done my work experience at the Port Erin Marine Laboratory, an internationally renowned research centre which was part of Liverpool University. The laboratory had a long history of fisheries research and advising the government with fisheries management, but in the late 1980s some of the scientists began to get more involved in the local marine management side of things and in promoting marine conservation. These marine biologists were instrumental in setting up the Calf Marine Trust, a group made up of scientists and members of the local community, to investigate protecting the Calf of Man. The Trust had a wide range of members with different expertise, including local community leaders. In 1992 the Calf Marine Trust put together a detailed and ambitious proposal for protecting the Calf as the Isle of Man's first Marine Nature Reserve.

The Calf of Man Marine Nature Reserve proposal outlined a suite of protection measures, including banning dredging and trawling for fish and shellfish within a 500-metre radius of the Calf. It also proposed allowing pot fishermen to continue to fish but to limit new potting activity and outlined measures to prevent disturbance of pupping seals and nesting birds. The plans were focused on preserving the Calf's spectacular marine life.

In the scientific surveys which informed the proposals, divers had recorded 449 species of animals and plants in total, 95 of which were considered of conservation importance and 30 which had never been found before in Manx waters. When compared to other sites in Scotland and Northern Ireland where similar surveys had been carried out, the diversity of the Calf of Man came out on top. During those surveys two glamorous new species of nudibranchs (sea slugs) were discovered. *Doto sarsiae* (these creatures are still a little too new and a little too niche to have common names yet) has a pale pink body with red speckles and its back is covered in flamboyant fluffy pink branchial plumes (external lungs for gathering oxygen). It has very specific requirements, feeding on a particular species of hydroid (a plant-like animal) called *Sarsia eximia* that lives on kelp stipes and rocky reefs in areas of high current. *Doto hydrallmaniae* is a little less striking, with a similar pale body speckled in red, but its branchial plumes are a khaki colour. It is no less fussy and only feeds on one species of hydroid, *Hydrallmania falcata*. Both species have since been discovered elsewhere but for a few years they were the Island's only endemic species (known only from there).

When I first read the Calf of Man survey reports I hadn't dived around the Calf myself. The lists of species were impressive and the photographs of the wispy strands of hydroids and ghost-like nudibranchs piqued my curiosity, but gave no sense of the spectacular, technicolour reefs I was missing out on. Beyond their scientific interest, the walls, caves and pinnacles of the waters around the Calf are well known as recreational dive sites and the Calf of Man is often named in top tens of dive locations in the Irish Sea, the British Isles and even Europe.

The Calf underwater is best known for its psychedelic walls of what is sometimes called animal turf, a phrase which somehow doesn't capture what a spectacle it can be. This fluffy covering of encrusting creatures leaves no visible trace of the underlying rock surfaces and creates seascapes of colour and vibrancy comparable to tropical coral reefs. The Manx slate that makes up most of the Calf's geology plunges on down from the steep cliffs and forms almost vertical underwater walls, scoured by roaring currents. These walls are encrusted on every centimetre with seventies-coloured assemblages of jewel anemones, bright sponges and other colonial animals like sea squirts and hydroids. On less steep surfaces more complex structures reach out into the currents to catch passing plankton. The white and orange protrusions of dead men's fingers are undeniably like hands. These soft corals look delicate and coral-like when they have their polyps out feeding on plankton from the current, but more macabre when their polyps are retracted and they are waxy white and a little bloated-looking. On other sloping surfaces are meadows of oaten pipe hydroids. These delicate structures are so like flowers it is difficult to believe they are animals. In the sea, stalked and rooted things that bloom and blossom are so often animals, it is easy to mistake them.

And it isn't just an exuberance of invertebrate life waiting to be discovered in these waters. While you dive among these living kaleidoscopes of colours and patterns, you are often accompanied by inquisitive grey seals. Some just hover and swirl gently in the background and you only see them when you get that feeling of being watched. Turn around quickly and you will catch them for a moment before they swim nonchalantly away, their enormous cartoon eyes meeting yours, a little sad that they've been caught, but unrepentant. Others are much more boisterous, the ones that divers talk about in pubs and feature in online videos that go viral. They wrestle with your dive fins (yellow ones are supposed to be particularly favoured, which I can confirm from personal experience). They nudge and pat and make sudden changes of direction that start the water swirling around both diver and pinniped (the seal and walrus family which can all spend extended time on land as well as in the sea). In some cases they've made swipes at masks, which is where it starts getting more alarming. But my experiences with the Calf's curious seals have only been good and they are some of the closest encounters with nature I've had, leaving me with a strong sense of the mischievous personalities of these creatures.

The Calf is a haven for seals. The best place to watch them from land is at the Sound, the southernmost tip of the Isle of Man that looks south over the Calf. On Kittlerland, a rocky islet about 500 metres across, up to a hundred seals (usually grey seals, but with the occasional common seal) can be hauled out at any one time at low tide. When you first look out to sea from the rabbit-grazed turf above the rocks you might think you'd missed them.

But look closer and you see their dark shapes, speckled with lighter patches so similar to the barnacles that freckle the dark rocks they favour. They shuffle together, nudging each other, sometimes companionably, other times less so. Those who have found small rocks to perch on as the tide retreats curl up at each end like bananas, leaving only their middle in contact with the rock. They gaze around, flapping the occasional flipper or scratching their heads. Seals are often described as dog-like, with their big eyes and playful behaviour underwater. Like many animals that live part of their time in air and part in water, they suffer from the indignity of appearing flabby and uncoordinated on land, shuffling about on their bellies to get comfortable, and rolling a little from side to side as if they can't quite get balanced. But underwater they are torpedo-like. Fast, sleek, streamlined and gone in a flash.

Grey seals around the Calf of Man, camouflaged on the rocks.

Around the quiet coves and beaches at the bottom of steep cliffs are seal nurseries. The Calf offers a wealth of undisturbed beaches and caves where they can birth their pups and leave them safely while they hunt for food and come back to feed them. White-furred baby seals are well known from posters and wildlife documentaries but in real life they surprised me. They are ridiculously fat and fluffy. Their mothers feed them up on the richest of milks for two to three weeks, setting them up for fending for themselves in our cool waters. They seem unfortunately conspicuous, with their white fur, but then when you see them on the beaches among quartzy pebbles and pale grey slate, their bright fur makes more sense.

It's not surprising that there were strong feelings over proposals to change anything about the magical Calf of Man, and the debate over the proposed Marine Nature Reserve was fierce. It is a place beloved by the people of the south of the Island, and highly esteemed by scientists. After years of public meetings and press articles, the proposal to protect the Calf of Man was abandoned. There are various narratives around what happened, but in short, a draft consultation version of the management plan was submitted to the government for consideration in 1991. At the time there was no capacity in government to deal with marine conservation and the document was put out to the public without any resource to help people understand the proposals or put forward their views. It seems that it was therefore seen by many as an idea by the non-Manx scientists at the marine laboratory that aimed to curtail the fishing activities of Manx fishermen. There were vocal and passionate advocates both for and against the plans and the discussions became heated. Without any mediation or government intervention it became an entrenched argument based largely on opinion, rather than informed by any bigger picture. After a voluntary Marine Nature Reserve was proposed instead of a legally protected designation, the issue eventually seemed to fizzle out, leaving a lot of people feeling aggrieved and alienated. It became a case study in how not to establish a protected area and highlighted the importance of investing time and resources in working with a community to make changes that will affect their way of life. But at least it highlighted the value of the Calf of Man and its marine life to the wider population.

Staff moved on from Port Erin Marine Laboratory and for a number of years no one working in the government or with the Manx Wildlife Trust was specifically focused on marine conservation. A parallel process, however, was having more success. In 1989 a scientist at the laboratory, Dr Andy Brand, had been studying the local king scallop fisheries for over twenty years. King scallops are large bivalves (two-shelled molluscs) that live on the seabed. They have one curved white shell (the ones that were used as ashtrays years ago) and one pink or brown flat shell. The old Manx fishermen didn't really fish for scallops and they weren't a popular food, until the 1930s and '40s when the fishery began to develop. But by the 1980s, it was a thriving part of the fishing industry on the Isle of Man. Because king scallops spend most of their lives snuggled down into the sand and gravel of the seabed, curved side down and flat side flush with the ground, they can't be fished using the trawls used for catching many species of fish. Instead, racks of strong metal teeth known as dredges are used to rake the king scallops off the seabed, along with everything else. It is a devastating process and one which, like many practices that continue to destroy habitats and lay waste to ecosystems, would not be developed as a new fishing technique today but had become accepted over time. Dr Brand and his team led pioneering work on the impact of this dredging on the seabed ecosystem and he worked with the government to get permission to close a small area of sea off Port Erin Bay to scallop dredging to provide an unfished comparison site to the areas that were regularly dredged. At the time, this was unpopular too and the area was regularly challenged by a small minority of disgruntled fishermen. However, because the area was closed for experimental purposes, the scientists, supported by the government, prevailed. Over the years the scientists at Port Erin Marine Laboratory worked with local fishermen, sharing their research results which showed increasing densities of king scallops in the closed area, spilling out into the surrounding fishing grounds. At the same time, the fishermen themselves gradually began to see an increase in the numbers and size of scallops just outside the closed area and would often fish right up to the boundary of the closed area to benefit from those scallops. Support for the scheme among the initially reluctant local fishermen began to grow.

In 2000 Dr Susan Gubbay, a well-known marine consultant based in the UK, was commissioned by the Manx Wildlife Trust to review potential sites for Marine Nature Reserves in the Isle of Man. Along with twelve other sites, she identified the Calf of Man as important, and described its rich and varied fauna and the wealth of internationally and nationally rare species. But, with the memory of the acrimony over the failed Calf designation still fresh in many people's minds, and with limited resources for marine conservation, nothing came of Dr Gubbay's excellent report.

So, this is where things were when I returned to the Island from studying and working abroad, brimming with enthusiasm about how effective marine protected areas could be to nurture marine life and help fishermen. There was the backdrop of the disappointing failure of communication and engagement in the Calf and the associated local tension and debate. However, there was also one emerging success with the Port Erin Closed Area which was yielding important science and gradually bringing the fishing industry on board with the concept of marine protected areas. But I had more driving me besides that. The Island was my home, and that of my ancestors (on one side at least) for many generations; it had shaped me in ways I was constantly discovering and I'd returned much sooner than I'd ever have imagined. The magnetic pull of islands on their escaped islanders seems to be a universal experience, wherever those islands are. You may spend years complaining about your limited horizons, the small scale of everything, the gossip and the inconvenience of travel. You will study or work hard to create your own particular escape route, but eventually you will return.

2

The Sweetest of Bays

'Seen from the sea it is a lovely thing to look upon, it never fails to bring me a thrill of the heart as it comes out of the distance. It lies like a bird on the waters. You see it from end to end, and from water's edge to topmost peak, often enshrouded in mists, a dim ghost on a grey sea; sometimes purple against the setting sun. Then, as you sail up to it, a rugged coast, grand in its beetling heights, on the south and west, and broken into the sweetest bays everywhere. The water, clear as crystal and blue as the sky in summer, you can see the shingle and the moss through many fathoms.'

Hall Caine, *The Little Manx Nation*, 1891

The Isle of Man was a wonderful place to grow up, with lots of time spent outdoors and especially on the beach. I spent most of my teenage years continuing to enjoy the sea and countryside, with walks on the coast with my family, going out in my dad's little rowing boat, staying with my grandparents in their seaside cottage and running down to the beach in under a minute. But at the same time I was desperate to leave and be where, as I saw it, things actually happened, so I could start my life.

'Never turn your back on the sea.' I was seven or eight years old when my dad gave me this advice. We were standing on the sloping pebble beach at Cornaa on a stormy day. Ever since, I've watched the sea and I've listened. I've been aware of its movements. I spent weeks every year in my grandparents' house perched above Port Erin Bay. There were fondant-coloured sea urchins among the best china and the roof beams in the attic had been salvaged from a shipwreck.

My dad was born in the Isle of Man to a Manx mother from a Port Erin fishing family and a Manx father who had grown up in a croft in the southern hills of the Island and whose father had been a lead miner in the Foxdale mines. Dad left the Island at eighteen to study physics at Liverpool University, a four-hour ferry trip away and a favourite place for Manx students. My dad loves the sea and he loves the Isle of Man and while he taught for over fourteen years in Liverpool, he spent as many holidays as he could back on the Island, and whenever possible on or near the sea, helping his uncles on their fishing boats or walking on the coastal paths that radiate from Port Erin. He met my mum in 1963 while he was at university. She grew up in Aintree and was working as a dental nurse in the dentist's he went to on Penny Lane. I loved that Beatles connection when I was growing up and the idea of my mum and her friend Anne watching the world go by from the dentist's window between patients, and my dad in his student donkey jacket walking along the wet pavement, part of the montage of suburban life. I still love Liverpool.

I was six when we moved to the Isle of Man. Dad was so keen to get back he took a demotion from head of science at a big Liverpool comprehensive to head of physics at a smaller school in Ramsey, the other end of the Island to where he'd grown up, and that's where we moved. At weekends we'd drive south to Port Erin, the full length of the Island in an hour. From my grandparents' house the views of the bay were ever-changing and we all kept watch for gannets diving, a new boat anchoring offshore and the ever-changing shape of the sea. Each day the tide revealed the tumbled wreck of the breakwater, then hastily covered it up again and through the year the sunsets slid across the horizon and disappeared behind Bradda Head.

At our home in the north of the Island I had another beach to explore. Ramsey is a small town that sits in the middle of a bay that extends, with its long curve of sand, from Gob ny Rona (Manx Gaelic for Seal Point) in the south to the Point of Ayre in the north. In the summer we camped out by the rusting arthropod legs of the Queen's Pier, a crumbling Victorian relic gnarled with clusters of blue mussels, and jumped in the waves as they rolled and crashed and streamed over the sand. On calm days we stood knee-deep like statues and watched the speckled juvenile plaice emerge from their sandy camouflage and make short dashes around our toes.

As teenagers my friends and I would gravitate to the shore to talk. We'd stride out towards the sea and keep our eyes on the horizon as we talked about where we would go and what we'd do. Walking back, we'd take in the town sprawled low between the sea and the dark bulk of North Barrule, the Island's second-highest peak, looming above. We planned our escapes. With boys, a walk across the beach, past the arches leading up to Ballure Glen and to the ribcage remains of the wrecked trawler could mean the beginning of something, or the end.

Dad in the 1960s at Port Erin harbour, where his grandfather and uncles kept their boats.

I decided early on that I wanted to be a marine biologist. My dad and my grandma told so many stories about the sea and when I was young I was sometimes allowed out on one of the great-uncles' boats to see those lobsters at their most surreally blue as they came out of the pots, and hearing that addictive 'thresh' sound as the pots were thrown back in. The great uncles were archetypal traditional Manx fishermen, with navy jerseys and caps, and red wind-burnt cheeks. Uncle Jack once featured on the front of the UK *Christian Herald*, stooped over his lobster pots on the harbour's edge.

Fish were my first real love and it was going out fishing for pollack (known locally as *callig*, the Manx Gaelic name) in my dad's little rowing boat, coming back and dissecting the fish before they were cooked for tea that really kindled my interest. It was also the long hours spent on the beach, which was what I remembered most about the school holidays we always spent on the Isle of Man before we moved back. I remember telling my best friend Ruth at primary school about the serendipity of the endless bays and coves and beaches, just like in our beloved Enid Blyton adventures. I don't know if it is something that all sea-lovers have, but I have one beach on the Isle of Man that I think of as my own. There are so many to choose from and we are lucky to have so many beaches and seemingly so few people visiting them at any one time. Their names are magical. There is the Dhoon beach at the bottom of a steep, waterfall-showered glen with a huge slab of slate plummeting into the sea at one side; Port Cornaa where the river winds through saltmarsh and emerges in an often visible halocline, where salt and freshwater separate into layers below the surface; Niarbyl beach and its view of layer upon layer of fading headlands south as far as the Calf. The name Niarbyl comes from the Manx Gaelic words for the tail, *yn arbyl*, from the tail of rocks diminishing out into the south-west sea. From the small beach with a few little thatched cottages and rockpools galore, you can head out among the rocks of the tail. At Niarbyl beach you can even stand on the point where ancient continents collided, part of the process of the ancient Iapetus Ocean disappearing, over 420 million years ago. And Lewaigue (pronounced Layg) and Port-e-Vullen, Laxey and Santon Gorge. As the novelist Hall Caine observed, our coastline is studded with the 'sweetest of bays'.

Spaldrick beach is tiny, around fifty metres wide and tucked around the corner from the wide sandy curve of Port Erin beach. Growing up we called the larger Port Erin beach 'the sandy beach' as opposed to Spaldrick and there would often be a debate about which one to go to. If you crossed the road from my grandmother's house it took little more than a minute to walk down some uneven and often overgrown steps to Spaldrick. You'd often find you had the pebbly beach to yourself. The sandy beach was a ten-minute walk along the promenade and on a hot day in the school holidays would be packed with families doing the traditional beach activities of deckchair sitting, ice-cream eating, sandcastle building and splashing in the shallows.

In red wellies, and usually wearing a red bobble hat too, and completely focused on a rockpool or a clump of kelp or something in the strandline, there are photos of me down Spaldrick beach from when I was first walking and almost every year since, business-like with my bucket and net, catching shrimps and then returning them, carefully overturning rocks to find crabs, scouring the tideline on Spaldrick beach for a chalky cuttlefish endoskeleton or a desiccated dogfish. When the tide is out the rockpooling and exploring on the beach is exciting. To the north side you can clamber over some rocks onto a raised rocky platform where my favourite childhood rockpool can be found. It was the best place to catch shrimps to observe in my little red bucket and then return to the pool. Among the rocks and boulders beyond the pool, where a stream makes its way down to the sea, juvenile eels could always be found sliding between the pebbles. If you managed to catch an eel, its slime would be left on your hands and your bucket, smelling of earth.

With my grandma rockpooling on Spaldrick beach.

Dragon-like in the middle of the bay is Betsy Donnag, a rocky centrepiece for the beach when the tide is out and home to a wonderful long rockpool that often has blennies and other little fish that freeze and peer up through clear water with bulging eyes. When the tide is in it is a great focus for snorkelling, swirling in ballan wrasse and bladder wrack. The boat rock to the right of the beach is a v-shaped rock mid-shore. It makes the perfect boat for pirate adventures. On a wild winter's day the waves rolling in from the south-west crash onto Betsy Donnag, casting spray far and wide. To the south side of the beach is a rocky cliff-side, breaking up into a winding path through rock faces to the old swimming pool. At low spring tides you can walk through a clicking, creaking labyrinth of barnacles, beadlet anemones and dripping bladder wrack and knotted wrack. Giant spider crabs can lurk in these sheltered alleys between sea and land, and orange and yellow sponges encrust the inside of each crevice in the rocks. At high tide you can snorkel through the same passageways and see the weed waving high off the seabed and wrasse weaving along with you as you make your way through to the open sea.

The strandline of Spaldrick is where we were always told my great-great-grandfather and his brother who built the house found a huge beam from a ship that became the supporting purlin still visible in the attic of my grandmother's house. Washed up in mounds of wrack can be found papery masses of whelks' eggs and translucent tortoise-shell mermaid's purses and the splintered remains of storm-torn seabirds. Decades before we all became focused on marine plastics, as a small child I became fascinated with the exotic

man-made bits and pieces you could find knotted up in
the blackening wrack. In the seventies there seemed so
little plastic on the beach. I went through a stage when
I stopped collecting interesting shells and other natural
beach-cast bits and bobs and started collecting the plastic.
The lids of unrecognisable brands of soft drink, milk cartons
with exotic alphabets. Little monochrome people from
cereal packets, a building block and a worn plastic tree. To
a six-year-old they seemed as treasure-like and valuable as
a buttercup-yellow periwinkle or an opal-lined top shell.

I spent so many days exploring Spaldrick beach, but
certain memories have stayed with me. I was around eight
years old and had just arrived at my grandparents' house
after the hour-long drive from Ramsey with my parents.
As I often did, I said a quick hello and then crossed the
road and ran down the winding, uneven steps to the beach.
I was alert to any changes since my last visit. Sometimes
the beach was piled high with mountains of freshly cast
weed. Other times it was hard to find any seaweed, but
the pebbles might have shifted into new formations, higher
up the beach, or scoured down to the rocks. When the
south-westerlies had been persistent, the beach would be
sprinkled with the primary colours of beach litter – green
milk cartons from Ireland, a yellow fisherman's welly, a red
plastic fuel drum and a blue fishbox embossed with the
name of a fishermen's co-operative in Kilkeel. Usually I
was the only person there and I would spend a little time
scouring the tideline for interesting finds. If the tide was
low I would watch for fish or shrimps in the rockpools;
if there was a big sea and the tide was high I might just
stand above the reach of the spray and watch the waves.

This time, as soon as I got halfway down the steps I noticed something large in the middle of the beach, on a heap of tangled brown weed. I picked up my pace and jumped from a few steps before the beach onto a patch of pebbles. As I made my way across the shingle, dotted with seakale, I began to smell something strong, unpleasant and slightly sweet. And then I saw it. A patchy-brown carcass, rubbed raw in some places but with head and fins intact. A seal, long dead. It was the first time I'd found a dead seal washed up on the beach, but because it had not been dead too long I recognised it immediately. I was distraught. The Christmas before I'd had my first taste of death. My grandfather's sister, Auntie Alice, who we'd visited in a Victorian old people's home where she always sat in the same corner with her friend, had passed away that winter. I thought of the small groups of curious, gentle seals we watched from our hiding place at Port Mooar and who watched us back, and the big raucous rabbles of seals at Kitterland that sometimes seemed to be performing to their human audiences at the Sound. I didn't explore any further that day. I turned and ran back up the steep steps, through the front door and up the red-carpeted stairs to the tiny bedroom I always stayed in at my grandparents' house. I shut myself in and kept looking down, trying to see the seal on the beach. Inconsolable. I've seen so many dead seals since then, and many other species of marine mammal, but that day has always stayed with me.

When I was fifteen years old, just beginning to find my own slightly goth style but still very square and strait-laced, I got to see a completely different side of Port Erin. There is a photo of me from that time – with little red hair clips with tiny silk roses holding back the wispy edges of my plait, a navy-blue cotton M&S jumper and a patterned Indian silk scarf.

I was doing work experience at the Port Erin Marine Laboratory. One of my enduring memories is a day spent wrist-deep in herring in a cool, wet lab as I learnt to remove their tiny ear bones, my lab coat spattered with blood. I didn't spend all my time indoors though. One day I went out on the lab's research vessel *Sula* (named after the old scientific name for gannet which is *Sula bassana* – it has since changed to *Morus bassanus*). Some of the team were diving and I sat on the boat and waited for them to surface again. One PhD student pointed out fulmars with their smoky eyes flying forays out from the southern cliffs. I'd never noticed them before. This was the late 1980s, and marine biology students in Port Erin wore Scandinavian jumpers and drove dilapidated cars with dive gear permanently stowed in the boot, or a surfboard on the roof. They were irresistibly glamorous to me at the time. In the 1980s the Isle of Man's finance sector was beginning to flourish, and one of my school friends did her work experience in an investment company and started tracking stocks and shares in the *FT*. I guess that seemed glamorous too. But glamour to me was the smell of running seawater, jumpers that hadn't been washed for a while, shirt cuffs dipped in herring blood, fish-scented hair, scallop gonads and seaweed samples. I had found my vocation.

I had known about the Port Erin Marine Laboratory for as long as I could remember. My grandmother loved to tell stories of how any interesting specimens that her father and brothers brought up in their pots or nets would be taken there for the 'winkle-pickers' at the biological station to have a look at. There was a small aquarium where locals and tourists could see some specimens of the Island's marine life up close. My great-grandfather reportedly delivered many a conger eel to the laboratory. Conger eels can grow to three metres or more in length, and have a big mouth, strong jaws and cold, beady eyes. My childhood sea-swimming experiences were clouded by a fear of the jaws of a conger fastened around my ankle as I swam across the bay.

A favourite story my grandmother told was about a rare albino lobster that her father caught in one of his pots, with a white shell instead of the luxuriant blue of the usual sort. This ghostly lobster was a star attraction in the aquarium for years.

The aquarium was painted black inside with around ten windows into small tanks. Seawater pumped in from the bay ran constantly between tanks holding fish and other creatures found in the surrounding waters and the floor always seemed to be wet. This tiny, low-key aquarium was a far cry from the glamour of today's big commercial aquaria, with their tunnels under the shark tanks and multistorey tanks displaying kelp forests or coral reefs. But they gave people who lived by the sea a much-needed glimpse underneath the surface and were hugely popular with locals and visitors alike. In the decades since the Port Erin aquarium closed, the access to living sea creatures has been restricted to annual marine days where marine biologists and divers collect sea creatures and display them in what used to be called touch tanks. These events have long been organised by the Manx Wildlife Trust and they are very popular with as many as 5000 people visiting over a weekend. The creatures can have a hard time though. They get warm in the tanks and they used to get a lot of handling from enthusiastic children (and adults). I am a big fan of more sustainable small-scale local aquaria. Some creatures do lose their liberty and probably meet untimely ends but they provide thousands of people with an insight into the sea. Conger eels and lobster are ideal occupants, because they don't do a huge amount but just watching their twitching antennae or sudden darting action can be very absorbing.

My grandmother often recalled the invasions of 'winkle-pickers', big groups of marine biologists scouring the rocky shores of Port Erin Bay or digging in the sand of Port Erin beach. She was born on the Island in 1913 and when she was growing up the marine laboratory would have had resident scientists and visiting groups from the UK. One of the marine scientists who wrote a key Manx marine biological text used to rent my grandmother's house at one point, and she spoke proudly about this.

My childhood was steeped in the maritime history of the Island. The benevolent spectre of the nineteenth-century naturalist Edward Forbes loomed large. A bust of his distinctive head (he seems to have sported an unusual bob for most of his life) was on display at the Port Erin Marine Laboratory when I did my work experience there – and I gravitated towards him and his story. Edward Forbes grew up on the Isle of Man, in Ballaugh, not far from where I had, and had gone on to become one of the first true marine biologists and oceanographers. He was born in 1815 and died aged just thirty-nine in 1854. But he wasn't just a pioneering, adventuring Manx marine biologist who travelled around the world discovering amazing things about the sea, describing new species (like the painted balloon aeolis, a nudibranch which he described in 1838) and having dozens of species named after him, including the European northern squid (*Loligo forbesii*). He was also a poet, an illustrator and a wonderful enthusiast. He is one of the people I would most like to have met. In marine circles he is now best known for his famously incorrect Azoic hypothesis, his theory that life could not exist below a depth of 300 fathoms (550 metres). This is such a shame because he got so much right. In particular, his pioneering work on biogeography – how species vary with location – still informs work on species around the British Isles today. Forbes showed an amazing capacity for scientific research even from a young age. In an account of his childhood by a friend of the family we hear how 'During his visits to his grandmother at Ballaugh, he was in the habit of going out in a small fishing-boat into the Bay, to an oyster-bank three or four miles distant from the shore, for the purpose of dredging for mollusca.'

This dredging work off the west coast of the Island would have given Forbes an amazing insight into the diversity of marine life and was to shape his career. It was a great source of inspiration to me, that someone who had grown up on the Island had gone on to be so influential in global marine science and it was nice to see Edward's familiar face looking down over the coffee room at the lab. It was a good sign.

★

Despite my love of the ocean, when I left the Isle of Man aged eighteen to start a biology degree at the University of York I had no intention of ever going back. In October 1991 I sailed from Douglas, the capital of the Isle of Man, to Heysham, in Lancashire, England. I travelled on the *Lady of Mann* ferry with a rucksack that I'd bought to go to the Reading Festival a couple of months before, and assorted bags. I'd sent my trunk ahead, the same one my dad had used when he'd left the Island to study.

My university choices were based on the opportunities they gave to travel. At York, I'd specifically chosen one of the few biology programmes that included a year abroad, and it also had a Tropical Marine Research Unit specialising in coral reef research. Having left the British Isles only once in my first eighteen years, I wanted to travel as widely and excitingly as possible.

In global terms, York isn't all that far from the sea but for a student without a car, a trip to Whitby or Scarborough was a rare occasion – usually only when someone was visiting me. But every holiday I travelled back by train across the Pennines and caught the ferry (we always just called it 'the boat') from Heysham or Liverpool. Up on deck I'd reacquaint myself with salt-spray, watching out for barrel jellyfish or porpoises. Once I saw a harbour porpoise swim slowly through the muddy wake of the boat as it manoeuvred out in the Mersey, beneath the austere gaze of the Liver Birds. On the deck I'd join the homesick fellow travellers picking out the grey smudge on the horizon that would transform with every nautical mile into our *Mannin veg veen* (our little Isle of Man).

In my second year at university I found myself even further from the sea, in the landlocked centre of western Europe, studying biology in Bavaria. On the map of Europe on my bedroom wall in the halls for foreign students I marvelled at the network of railway routes at my disposal. Just a train journey away from Budapest, Madrid or Copenhagen – so exciting for an island girl. But on darker days I couldn't help notice that the edges of the Baltic and the Mediterranean were so far away. Next to the map I had Blu-Tacked a print of Waterhouse's *A Mermaid*, looking unhappy as small waves broke a short distance from her neat, silvery tail. My mum would post me dull green bars of seaweed soap and in the orange Formica shower room I'd momentarily scent the Irish Sea in processed flakes of kelp.

I was nineteen when I saw my first coral reef. I had travelled to Egypt with my new university friend Rachel who was also studying biology, staying with friends of hers in Cairo and then travelling to Luxor to visit the Valley of the Kings and then to the Sinai Peninsula and the Red Sea. With a mask and snorkel, the clear waters revealed a landscape I could never have imagined. In our black school swimming costumes we drifted out over the reef above the Blue Hole at Dahab in Egypt and I couldn't believe it was real. In a coastal café, we sat on the floor and ate parrotfish, discovering that even their bones were an exotic blue.

The prospectus research paid off and I managed to get an undergraduate research project with the Tropical Marine Research Unit, supervised by the director, Dr Rupert Ormond. Travelling back to Egypt two years later to do research for my dissertation in the Ras Mohammed National Park, I learnt to dive, a whole new enchantment. Among car-sized Napoleon wrasse and humphead parrot-fish bigger than me, I could fly over coral gardens, and then glide down into gullies, just by breathing out. I spent weeks snorkelling on small areas of reef flat (the shallows on the top of a coral reef) following individuals of two species of butterflyfish, the raccoon butterflyfish and the threadfin butterflyfish, to map their territories and record their interactions. Another York undergraduate, Becca, and I were assisting two PhD students with their work and carrying out our own research projects. We camped in the Sinai desert and walked straight into the sea each morning, each to our own study site where we'd snorkel for hours on our own (expedition health and safety has moved on quite a bit in the intervening years). I'd never spent so much time actually underwater and I became part of that little reef community, recognising each cave and outcrop of coral and distinguishing between the fish I was studying by tiny fin nicks or imperfections in the patterns on their flanks. By the end of the project I felt as though I knew my fishy subjects as individuals, and could mimic their displays and quirks, as they darted between feeding on coral polyps or fragments of dead jellyfish and frightening off intruders who dared to venture over the invisible boundaries of their territories.

The joy of fieldwork and then writing up my research gave me a real taste for marine science and I decided that I definitely wanted to continue with my studies and move on to a PhD.

*

The first time I remember really looking at seagrass was perched at the front of a small boat sailing round to Kilindoni, the main settlement on Mafia, a small island off the coast of Tanzania in East Africa. The water was calm and clear. The seabed passed below us like a natural history documentary on fast forward: coral reef – sand – a big bamboo fish trap – the dark shape of a huge ray passing like a detached shadow. And then world maps of green, hazed in fish and flecked with cartoon-coloured starfish – tropical seagrass meadows. In deeper waters the meadow was just a green blur but as we entered the shallows, I could make out the dense clumps of swaying straps of green and ragtag schools of numerous different species of fish all shoaling together, some bright like reef fish, but many grey and green and yellow, well suited to the dappled meadow they sheltered in.

Less than an hour before, the boat I'd been passenger on had sunk and now lay twenty metres below, just off the coral reef. The journey so far (we'd been at sea for ten days) had been challenging. We had been heading south against the monsoon winds, so we tended to anchor up during the day and sail at night when the winds were lighter. Every night we seemed to run aground or get caught in a storm. We had no phones or radios or any way of making contact with anyone. To make tea or cook, one of us would have to hold the charcoal stove, balancing in the bowels of the dhow (a traditional wooden Indian Ocean sailing boat), while another held the kettle or cooking pot. The coconut-palm roof of the boat was full of cockroaches that scuttled out at night and swarmed over our grubby white-sheet sleeping bags. There were no toilet facilities of any kind, and as the only woman on board I had developed complex rituals to preserve a shred of dignity as I hung over the side. The vessel's previous use had been to ferry cement between Dar es Salaam and Zanzibar – it wasn't really designed for passengers. After ten long days and terrifying nights at sea, our sinking was a remarkably undramatic affair. On a sunny morning after a stormy night, we were anchored offshore from Mafia Island, about 120 kilometres south of Dar es Salaam where our journey had begun, and the anchor began to drag and we were moving rapidly towards a reef. By the time the complicated sails were up, it was too late and we had hit the reef. Pete, the dive co-ordinator for the project, organised us to try to push the boat off the reef using the long poles we had on board. At around the same time the captain must have worked out that the tide was out and he could still wade to shore, so that's what he did. The rest of the crew stayed with us and the boat to try to save it. A motorboat passed in the distance and I frantically waved it down with a colourful sarong. We couldn't work out if they could see us, but it didn't slow down and it didn't come and rescue us. The hull must have been holed and began to fill up with water, so we moved some of the trunks and boxes up onto the deck and some of them onto the reef crest but the tide was rising and they were soon submerged. We were standing on top of the reef with the sea reaching our knees and rising and water pouring into the boat, and eventually someone (and it wasn't me) took the call to give up on the boat and try to reach the shore. By then there was no hope of walking to shore, and we even struggled to swim in the strong current that ran parallel to the shore. I had my diving fins tied around my waist with a sarong, which wasn't much use, and a few essentials like my walking boots and passport in my rucksack. Somehow, we all made it to the shore and everyone was safe. Pete knew the island well and set off almost immediately into the undergrowth behind the beach to find a nearby village. The crew headed off separately. Just after he'd gone, when it was just Alex, the other expedition staff member, and me sitting on the beach looking out to sea, the boat suddenly sank from view and we were left looking at a deceptively calm cobalt sea.

Pete returned with an ancient-looking old man who very kindly took us to the main settlement in his tiny open boat. We left the seagrass beds behind as we entered Kilindoni harbour and stepped ashore. A crowd had gathered to watch as we squelched up the beach in front of the village. We clutched small bags containing our essentials and nothing else. I had a ruler. Alex had a tin of condensed milk. Peter had some of his dive kit repair tools.

That journey over the shallow waters of Mafia Island, and those mottled expanses of seagrass, have stayed with me for over twenty-five years. I felt a mixture of relief at being on the boat, rather than in the water; exhaustion after the adrenalin of fighting to save the boat and attract the attention of rescuers (who never came), and wonder at the condensed lesson in marine biology and the sheer size of that ray. But I didn't know at the time how important those marine grasses would become to me.

The people of Kilindoni were very kind to us. Women at the little hotel we found our way to lent me bold fish-patterned sarongs with Swahili slogans printed around the hems to wrap around myself while they dried our clothes around a cluster of charcoal burners. The hotel owner ironed our passports and money dry. The chief of police helped me choose replacement clothes in the tiny village market, while we waited a few days for him to sign our shipwreck papers. In the tiny hotel room I'd wake up every night scrabbling at the door, convinced I was still on the boat and trapped below in a storm.

Three days after watching the mast of our project boat disappear beneath the reef breakers, we were flying north in a tiny passenger plane, passing over mangroves, reefs and the chocolate waters where the Rufiji Delta meets the Indian Ocean, and then on by motorboat to Quirimba Island in Mozambique, where I would encounter seagrass again. This time I was travelling with Pete, Alex and a group of paying volunteers who were joining the project. Some were on gap years, others were biologists who were keen to get work experience, and they were all excited to get to Quirimba.

When we realised that the coral reef diving that had been a key part of the project was not going to be possible initially (losing the boat was going to have a big impact), we had to find other ways of gathering useful information on the island's marine life and also keep the volunteers busy. We went down to the local fish landing site and got to know the fishermen, and began to go out fishing with them. My Mozambican colleague, marine botanist Mario, made initial contact with the fishermen and one captain agreed to us going out on his boat. The first trip was on a boat from Quiwandala, the fish landing site in the mangroves about an hour's walk from our camp. We sailed for about thirty minutes into the channel between Quirimba Island and mainland Mozambique and began fishing in surprisingly shallow water – not even waist deep. They spread a patched-together net out over about fifty metres and then hauled it back into the boat and a cascade of fish poured into the bilges. I have to admit that at first they didn't look exciting – a lot of greens and browns, and generally quite small. But on closer inspection this leaping green mass of life was an incredible mix of fish. I later identified over 250 different species from those catches, much more diverse than many coral reef fishery hauls.

On a fishing boat off Quirimba Island, Mozambique, assessing the catch of seagrass fish.

That first day I brought back a selection to identify and it took me many weeks to get to know all of the common species. Some of them were familiar to me from other coral reefs I had dived on, like the haughty-looking emperors in slight variations on the silver theme, and the spotted sweetlips or grunt. Others were completely new, specially adapted to seagrass like the perfectly camouflaged mottled seagrass parrotfish or the dirty grey faintly spotted African rabbitfish. There were twenty-six different species of wrasse alone, from the distinctive cream and black juveniles of coral reef favourites humphead or Napoleon wrasse, to three delicately patterned species of ribbon wrasse, known as *shingu* in Kimwani, the language of the Mwani people of the northern Mozambican coast.

As I got to know the fishermen and spent more time out on their boats in the shallow expanses of the Montepuez Channel, I began to realise just how important seagrass was for their livelihoods. I could talk with the fishermen in a mixture of Portuguese and Kimwani. Most boys on Quirimba went to school and learnt Portuguese. At that time, most girls didn't get the opportunity to go to school at all and so most women I met on the island didn't speak Portuguese. Most people in the islands also spoke other local languages: Swahili, which is spoken across Tanzania and Kenya to the north, and Makua, generally spoken inland and further south down the Mozambican coast. I got to know the women more slowly as I tried to learn Kimwani. Many of them spent low tides collecting *ombay*, cockle-like arc shells, and the local delicacy *macaza*, a species of fan shell among the intertidal seagrass meadows on the shore. On one low-tide foray, my friend Awaje

47

patiently showed me how to search for the bivalves using my bare toes to feel for the shells in the soft sand and mud between the seagrass. The women I met were expert in this and seemed to find shells to collect wherever they explored with their feet. I was less successful but it was exciting when my toes did make contact with one of the sought-after species.

I was privileged to get to know many of the boat captains and their crew. Most were friendly and seemed to enjoy having me and the volunteers on board. One of the crew would spot something interesting and leap off the boat to show it to us. Another would quiz me on the Kimwani names of the hundreds of species of fish they caught from the seagrass meadows, which came in very useful as I learnt more about the species, their behaviour and their uses.

Other captains allowed me on board but made it clear what an inconvenience it was and would constantly be getting me to move out of the way, even though making myself as unobtrusive as possible was my first priority. It wasn't an easy life for the fishermen. On one trip an unlucky captain managed to encounter one of the long-spined black sea urchins that live among the seagrass and stood waist deep in water shouting orders with pencil length spines still sticking out of his arm, like a human pin cushion.

It became clear as I got to know the fishermen that it was the sheltered, shallow, easily accessible seagrass beds that they depended on. The calm seagrass meadows with their hidden schools of fish, so much less showy than their coral reef counterparts, became my focus, and would later become something of an obsession.

Seagrasses are flowering, rooted plants that grow either entirely underwater or on the shore. Biologically they are very different from seaweeds, and much more similar to land plants. Seagrass habitats have long lived in the shadow of the glamorous coral reefs they are often so inextricably linked with in the tropics. Until very recently, seagrass beds had not attracted much attention outside marine science, but their ecological importance in tropical marine ecosystems has long been acknowledged. Indeed, they are often portrayed as part of a dynamic trinity of marine habitats all interacting and interdependent – coral reefs, seagrass beds and mangroves. Juvenile coral reef fish often live in seagrass beds and mangroves, moving from these safe nursery areas onto coral reefs as they mature. But until I started working with the fishermen of Quirimba, I'd never heard about seagrass beds being important for fisheries in their own right. On Quirimba Island almost everyone I met had some link to the seagrass meadows. Many men worked on the fishing boats that fished exclusively in the seagrass meadows of the channel. Many women collected shellfish from the other species of seagrass that grew on the shore. Others dried fish and shellfish and sold it to traders on the mainland. When the fishing boats returned to Quiwandala, the little sheltered port among the mangroves would be crowded with people and dozens of women and girls would wade out to the boats. Their faces were often painted white with a thick paste called *mussiro*, a Mozambican coastal tradition. They would have aluminium cooking pots balanced on their heads filled with coconut or peanut sweets which they traded with the fishermen for fish.

Seagrass meadows are of vital importance ecologically, socially and economically all around the world, including in the UK. But an appreciation of their importance has not been immediately translated into protection and seagrass habitats are continuing to decline globally. Threats to tropical seagrasses include coastal and marine developments, where habitat is lost as areas are cleared for hotels and shrimp farms.

I spent two long field trips in the Quirimbas Archipelago, and after that rocky start was able to collect useful data on the seagrass fisheries and later dive in the seagrass beds to understand the ecology of the habitat that sustained the fishery. I spent another year analysing the data and writing up and finally completing my PhD. My first job after that focused on tropical marine ecology and gathering the information needed to inform the design of marine protected areas. In the waters of the British Virgin Islands and Jamaica I once again encountered bewitching marine life and worked with fishermen to understand their fisheries and how MPAs might be able to help them.

Later I began a global review of how marine protected areas can boost local fisheries which was commissioned by the World Wide Fund for Nature (WWF). I became convinced of the value of well-designed marine protected areas not only to protect marine life, but also to help coastal communities have more resilient fisheries. It is now widely accepted that MPAs can play an important role in sustainable management of fisheries but in the early 2000s they were still seen as a threat to fisheries and local fishermen and women. In fact, there are many ways in which protected areas can help sustain fisheries. They protect nursery areas for young fish and shellfish, and they provide refuges for marine creatures to grow to large sizes which in turn allows them to produce more offspring. Because the vast majority of marine fish and shellfish spend part of their life cycle as tiny plankton, at the mercy of the ocean currents, the benefits of marine protected areas spread much further than their own boundaries and the increased numbers of planktonic young produced can boost populations a few metres away, and up to thousands of kilometres away, depending on the length of time the species spends as part of the plankton and how far that enables them to travel.

Diving on coral reefs in St Lucia.

By 2003 I had been living the exciting, well-travelled life I had aspired to growing up in the Isle of Man. However, I was becoming increasingly disillusioned with the carbon footprint of all the flying I was doing and also the ethics of doing what could now be called 'parachute science', scientists turning up, doing their thing and disappearing again, potentially bringing very little benefit and possibly some level of impact or damage to the community and ecosystem they'd spent time in (although the projects I worked on were always collaborations with local scientists and managers and I hope made positive contributions to the communities and environment I was privileged to work in). And I had realised how much there was to do closer to home, particularly back in the Isle of Man. Reflecting on my research experience on small tropical islands which all, surprisingly perhaps, had their similarities to my own island, I began to think about returning there, for a short time at least. I saw a job advertised at the Port Erin Marine Laboratory where I had done my work experience all those years ago. I applied and got the job. After twelve years away, I was going home.

3

The King of the Sea

'The Fish had a strong notion to make *Brac Gorm*, the Mackerel, king. He knew that, and he went and put beautiful lines and stripes on himself – pink and green and gold, and all the colours of the sea and sky. Then he was thinking diamonds of himself. But when he came he looked that grand that they didn't know him. So they said that he was artificial and would have nothing to do with him. In the end it was *Skeddan*, the Herring, the Lil Silver Fella, who was made King of the Sea.'

Sophia Morrison, *Manx Fairy Tales*, 1911

'No herring, no wedding.'

Old Manx proverb

It is 2004 and I'm on the deck of the *Aora* in the Firth of Clyde. Everyone stops to watch as the catch of herring is landed. Nothing has prepared me for the cascading sheets of silver that pour from the bulging net. It is hard to think of them as fish. They are a glittering, gleaming waterfall of silver. Now I can understand why in the British Isles and beyond the herring were once so revered. The songs and stories inspired by a little bony fish all make complete sense. Coming across a huge school of herring and catching them is like a fairytale; a haul of living treasure flickering and shining with good fortune and prosperity. A net full of herring is nature too beautiful and bounteous to believe.

The journey to catch these herring had been challenging and had given me an opportunity to empathise with my forefathers too. I was thirty and working at Port Erin Marine Laboratory, partly as a lecturer in marine conservation and fisheries and also on a European herring project, with partners around the British Isles and further afield. We'd travelled to Scotland by ferry then on to the little island of Cumbrae near Arran. We'd set off from Millport Marine Laboratory really early, just after five a.m. I'd rushed getting up and had broken my own golden rule of seafaring – always have breakfast. Once on board I'd realised that some of the sample containers hadn't been labelled so I went down into the lab area to carry on with that as the boat got ready to set sail. The boat was already lurching violently before we set off which didn't bode well. The forecast wasn't great, but the captain was happy to get going. We had a long sail before we reached the fishing site.

Sorting the herring catch on the deck of the research vessel.

Alongside that astonishing, eye-widening encounter with a shoal of captured herring, I remember two other things about that trip. The first is my shame and surprise at finding that I could actually get seasick. I'd spent lots of time on boats in all sorts of sea conditions literally from birth. I'd felt tired and drained after long nights on rough crossings but I'd never felt nauseous or that I was in any way impaired or debilitated. This sailing was different. Not long after finishing the labels, when we'd set off into the

Clyde, I began to feel terrible. I remembered all the times I'd been the one person not to get sick and how I'd had no idea what the others were suffering. But I managed to keep going and do what I needed to do. It wasn't a complete disaster but it was a humbling experience and it has made me much more wary and careful ever since. I felt like I'd lost a superpower.

But more memorable even than my first experience of seasickness was discovering Ailsa Craig.

It is a child's drawing of an island, a steep grey triangle rising out of the sea. Encountered on this silvery grey stormy morning as we made our way south, Ailsa Craig was like a wonder of the world. A few hundred metres away the air around the boat began to get busier with the white wingspans of gannets flying in all directions to and from the rock. The noise began too, a clattering, squawking bustle. I was not convinced at first that the white I could see on the rock was birds. I tried to distinguish between guano and nests and the birds themselves, but the more I looked the more birds I realised there were. The geology of Ailsa Craig is perfect for a huge gannet hotel; the granite slopes seem to be sheared into little bird-sized niches and it is just right to fit in plenty of animals while giving them all a suitable perch. I could have sat offshore Ailsa Craig all day and watched that busy community coming and going and jostling for space and calling to each other.

The project I was working on at the Port Erin Marine Laboratory was a European-funded study of herring populations around Europe to understand better the distinct shoals and their breeding patterns and migration routes. My role was to coordinate the Isle of Man sampling.

We had to collect a range of samples of herring from particular locations and times in the Irish Sea and then process the herring samples to send off to experts around Europe. One of the things we had to do took me back to my fifteen-year-old self doing work experience at Port Erin. We had to remove the tiny ear bones, known as otoliths, from 250 fish for each sample, and carefully store them for further study. Traditionally, otoliths have been used to age fish because they provide a mini record of the life of the fish, preserved in calcium carbonate and sometimes visible with the naked eye as rings or ridges. Science has now gone way beyond just the counting of rings for ageing of fish, and these samples were going to be analysed to detect heavy metals and other revealing chemicals that could tell the scientists where those herring may have spent their planktonic phase and juvenile months. The otolith chemistry as it is called is like a passport stamped with the places a fish has travelled and what it has eaten during its short life. I find locating and extracting the tiny, fiddly otoliths of herring very satisfying but even I found removing 250 over the course of a day or night (depending on when we got our hands on the herring) quite challenging.

The other samples we took were stomach parasites, to understand if genetically different herring had different sets of parasites living inside them. I was amazed at the number of worms you could find in a fish stomach if you looked. Clips of those silvery fins were also taken to be used for genetic analysis. I was particularly fascinated by the herring's hearts. Little meaty-looking cubes of red, they were strangely beautiful.

WestHer fish-id: 3-S06A-001 Roagan/Irish Sea/6 30/09/03

One of the hundreds of herring we studied.

Herring have a very special place in the hearts of Manx people. There is evidence that people were fishing for herring around the Isle of Man as early as the thirteenth century, and as a small subsistence fishery grew to an industrial scale in the nineteenth century, herring became essential to Manx life. In 1879 it was estimated that 1000 boats were fishing for herring in the waters between the Isle of Man and Ireland. Spuds and herring formed the staple diet for generations of Manx people and wealth from the herring fishery, which at its height was exporting large quantities of herring to the UK, Spain, Italy and further afield, is what some of our towns were built on. At the height of the herring fishery, for the latter half of the nineteenth century, the harbours around the Island would have been packed full of herring fishing boats and the quaysides lined with thousands of barrels of herring, but by the 1930s the boats fishing for herring could be counted in the tens rather than the hundreds. Herring is one of those species it really should be possible to fish sustainably. They mature quickly and produce large numbers of young and if they are not overfished and their special spawning grounds (where they lay sheets of eggs onto gravel and vegetation rather than releasing them into the current) are protected, it should be possible to fish them with minimal impact on the environment. However, they have also been subject to big natural variations in numbers, which can lead to overfishing as fishing capacity is built in response to a good year and then too much effort damages populations in subsequent years.

It was exciting to return to the Isle of Man to work on this iconic species and a big change from the tropical fish species in seagrass beds and coral reefs which I had specialised in previously. On this new project I spent days at sea, catching herring for the project, and revelled in the shimmering hauls as they showered onto the deck. I worked through the night up to my elbows in blood to dissect the samples and package up the different body parts for further analysis. I waited on the beach with baskets while a lone fisherman rowed his tiny boat round the bay with a net to drive the herring to shore. The herring that come into Port Erin Bay in the summer may have travelled long distances in their short lives.

I loved the smell of the marine laboratory; seawater on tap, fragments of seaweed in the cracks in the floor, tanks of fish and shellfish bubbling and frothing happily.

Undercurrents of fish left too long on a bench and fish waste bins that aren't cleaned out as often as they should be. There may also be a hint of high-proof alcohol being used for specimens, and in my lab time the cloying smell of formalin too. In my experience, marine laboratories, from Jamaica to Scotland, smell curiously similar and always evoke those first days I spent truly immersed in marine science.

On my first morning working at Port Erin Marine Laboratory, I cycled down the promenade from my cottage in Spaldrick, just outside Port Erin, to the lab and I thought I'd got the wrong day, the wrong time – it couldn't be 8.30 a.m. on a Monday. The promenade was deserted and no one passed me in a car. I had that panicked feeling that your clock has gone wrong, you've missed something important, like a bank holiday. After cycling daily through York's rush-hour traffic, my solitary cycle through the village felt very odd. But it was a fresh autumn day; there was a breeze from the south-west, the prevailing wind that seems to blow most of the year straight into Port Erin Bay. I knew this from growing up on the Island, but there really never seems to be much point spending a lot of time on your hair in the Isle of Man. Whatever I did, it was blown and blustered as soon as I left the house.

When I worked there, Port Erin Marine Laboratory was a place in limbo. The building had not been well maintained and there was a feeling of neglect – the paint peeled on the old building that had housed the aquarium and, at the back of the building, assorted abandoned experiments and equipment were strewn, rusting, rotting and mouldering. Part of this is de rigueur for a marine laboratory, but Port Erin in 2003 went beyond that. There was also a sense of a lot of the staff coming to the end of long, successful careers. When I joined the lab there was a cohort of male academics nearing retirement who in most cases had spent much of their working life at Port Erin.

My job was to lecture about marine conservation and fisheries management. I also taught general marine biology on the field courses for students visiting from Liverpool. The most memorable one was the Easter fieldtrip for the second-year students. This fortnight fieldtrip was the first big immersion in marine biology that many of the students got after a year or so of theory. They learnt how to survey sandy beaches for burrowing life, how to study the distribution of species on rocky shores and how to net juvenile fish in the shallows to determine which species were using a bay as a nursery area. It was wonderfully hands-on.

The beauty, elegance and diversity of fish are definitely part of what attracted me to marine biology in the first place. From an early age I've also been fascinated by the inner workings of fish – their delicate otoliths suspended clean and white in their fluid-filled cavity, the swim bladder that helps to maintain its position without sinking to the bottom or floating to the top, the gills fading from vivid red. I dearly wanted to convey that love and wonder to generations of students. But under the circumstances of that fieldtrip, I may have failed.

One of my tasks in preparing for the Easter fieldtrip was to source a good range of species of fish specimens for dissection. To reduce the number sacrificed unnecessarily it was good to source fish, if possible, that would otherwise be wasted. I spoke to Norman Sansbury, the last fisherman in Port St Mary still catching fish rather than shellfish, and sourced some big examples of cod and other fish from him. Then I went up to Peel and spoke to the prawn fishermen on their boats, tied up after a night trawling for *Nephrops* from the deep-water mud to the west of the Isle of Man.

I should mention a little bit about *Nephrops*. They are creatures of many names. You might know them best as scampi but, bread-crumbed and deep-fried they are completely unrecognisable as the wonderful pink hard-shelled prawns that live in complex burrows in soft mud and have a fascinating life cycle. They are better known as langoustine and also as Dublin Bay prawns and *Nephrops* (the first part of their Latin name, *Nephrops norwegicus*, which means 'kidney-eyed' because of their kidney-shaped eyes that resemble two glossy black beans on the end of stalks).

They are caught in two main ways. The most sustainable method is using pots, called creels, which targets larger adults and has minimal impact on the seabed. This method captures more male prawns; the females spend more time in their burrows in the seabed, brooding their eggs, so are less likely to be caught. The other way that *Nephrops* are caught is much less sustainable. Bottom trawls (nets which are dragged along the seabed) are used to disturb the muddy seabed where they live and catch them, along with dozens of different species of fish that also live in that habitat. The catches were often less than a quarter prawns and three-quarters unwanted fish, also known as by-catch, which until recently were mainly dumped, dead or dying, at sea. Regulations now require by-catch of fish which are under the legal minimum size to be recorded and returned to shore where they can be sold, not for human consumption but for other less valuable uses such as pet food or fishmeal production. These relatively new rules have helped reduce this terrible waste, or collateral damage, but it is still an issue in trawl and dredge fisheries globally. In my search for unwanted by-caught fish which could be made use of, the prawn boats were ideal, but from the point of view of fisheries sustainability they still leave a lot to be desired.

I collected the fish from the prawn trawlers and added them to my collection for the second-year practical. The day before the practical one of the technicians let me know that the freezers had gone off over the weekend and all my fish samples had defrosted. I had a quick look at them and made the call that while some of them had definitely seen better days, most of them would still be OK to dissect. It probably wasn't the right decision. By the time the students got the fish and the practical had been introduced, most of the fish were decomposing and smelt very bad. As a fish lover and someone who spent two years of my PhD almost constantly immersed in dead fish and fish guts I have quite a high tolerance level for fishy smells, but even I was beginning to recoil. We soldiered on, identifying the swim bladders, removing otoliths, examining livers and gills and mouth structure. But it was fish carnage and by the end of the session I don't imagine that many fish lovers remained.

During my year at the Port Erin Marine Laboratory, Liverpool University took the decision to close the lab down. The action was very much in line with the sad loss of field stations around the UK and further afield. In the early 2000s, outposts like Port Erin were increasingly being seen as expensive extras that couldn't be justified in the new business-like approach that universities were having to take, rather than as essential elements of training the next generation of marine biologists, naturalists and ecologists.

It was a terribly sad time. For the people who had been working at the lab for a long time, there was the uncertainty around redundancy and what they would do next. There was also much sorrow around the end of such an illustrious period of internationally renowned marine science. And around the Island, people who had never had anything to do with the lab, but who had liked the idea it was there, were sad to see it go, and with it the romance of marine biology. The announcement of the closure was also a very personal loss for me. It had been such an important place for me as a child, a teenager and then in forming my career. It appeared in so many of my grandmother's stories about Port Erin – whether it was about the aquarium, the relatives that worked at the laboratory over the years or the colourful characters that came to live in Port Erin to work there over more than a century. The place had an almost mythical status in my childhood and it was devastating to be there at the time when the decision was taken to close it down.

It felt like the end of an era for the lab's herring research and that felt personal too. Migratory fish have played an important part in my family history. My great-grandfather's horizons stretched beyond Port Erin Bay when he joined the fleets of small fishing boats following the herring and mackerel down through the Irish Sea and beyond, and tantalising little glimpses of those adventures could still be found in my childhood. While the herring fishery in Manx waters was usually limited to June to September, earlier in the year mackerel could be caught off the east of Ireland, so many Manx fishermen made the journey south to fish out of Kinsale, in the Republic of Ireland. Years ago I visited Kinsale, and alongside the Lusitania Museum, where I learnt about the tragic sinking of the passenger ship *Lusitania* just a few miles off Kinsale in 1915, I also saw many graves of Manx fishermen. I later learnt that a Manx fishing boat, *The Wanderer*, had been one of the first on the scene, rescuing 160 people from the water.

My great-great-uncle Edward Crebbin selling fishing tackle in Port Erin.

In the front room of my grandma's house at Spaldrick (she called it the parlour and only used it when there were guests) was an old-fashioned glass-fronted display cabinet where she kept all her best china and family heirlooms, interspersed by the cleaned-up spineless sea urchin shells retrieved from fishing boats. When I was a child, my favourite ornaments were two Victorian-looking ladies with tragic expressions, clutching delicate lacy handkerchiefs. They stood next to two little porcelain sailing ships. I always assumed they were a set and the ladies were weeping as their beloved sailed off across the ocean, but I realised much later that they were from completely different eras. There was also a set of pale-yellow fruit dishes painted with orange flowers with a matching serving bowl which my grandmother had won in a rowing race across the bay. I've got these now and we use them regularly, so they probably won't last another hundred years.

The oldest item, and the most fascinating to me as a child, was an old china mug with 'A present from Kinsale' in faded gold calligraphy script. My grandmother's grandfather brought it back for her when she was a girl in the 1920s, but I'd love to know the whole story of the mug. I try to imagine my great-great-grandfather, leaving his ship *The Black Hawk* tied up in harbour, taking some hard-earned cash and venturing into the village of Kinsale while he waits for the next tide for fishing. The stretch of Irish Sea between the Isle of Man and Kinsale must have been well known to Manx fishermen over centuries.

Grandma as a girl on Port Erin beach.

Many of the Isle of Man's towns were built on the herring industry (along with smuggling, which has been well studied, and slavery, which we're only really just beginning to acknowledge properly). One of those towns is Peel, which is still a fishing town and still has some of the grand houses built with herring money. They are surrounded by big gardens, some built of the red Peel sandstone, the only part of the Island where this can be found.

There are countless old photographs of the harbour in Peel full of herring fishing boats and barrels up and down the quay. In 1823 there were 250 herring boats in the Manx fleet. Now, there is no commercial fishery for herring at all. Like many fishing stories, the lack of herring is not solely down to overfishing. It is more complex than that. The herring spawning ground to the east of the Island is studied by fisheries scientists from Northern Ireland and fished by Northern Irish vessels. Until recently, a small-scale fisherman in Port Erin continued to catch small amounts of herring by rowing a seine net around in the bay and these would be landed for local consumption, but as many fish stocks are now managed across borders, Manx fishermen don't have quota (the necessary allocation which must be bought by a fisherman) to fish for herring, which has been a source of local sorrow in the past.

In terms of what has happened to the herring stocks, the story is more complex. Herring were always something of a boom-and-bust stock, flooding the market one year and yielding very little the next. But there was an element of overfishing that led to the decline of the Irish Sea fishery. Like many species, the health of herring population is also determined by the health of the seabed. Herring don't spawn into the water column, releasing their eggs to the perils of the open sea. They spawn above the seabed, depositing ribbons of eggs that stick to gravel and rocky bottoms. The young herring hatch from eggs which are firmly attached.

Herring can either feed on larger planktonic creatures, like copepods, by pecking them out of the water column with their extendable mouths, or just open their mouth and filter-feed like tiny baleen whales, if prey concentrations are high enough.

The biology of the herring has always captivated me as much as its beauty and wonder. I thought about this as I dissected herring for the project. It was my dad who made me love the sea by taking me out fishing, and onto the beach and walking beside the sea. And when we caught fish I would dissect them to find out what was inside before we had them for tea. Understanding how they worked made me love them even more, and I was still happy to eat them later.

I suppose this sums up the complexity of my relationship with the sea and the wider human experience too. We love the sea because of its beauty and the resonance of a sea view with something primeval within us. We enjoy interacting with it, whether that means kayaking with seals or reeling in a mackerel or the thrill of wading into the stinging cold of a winter sea and then plunging in. We have exploited, and potentially enjoyed, the sea for thousands of years.

I first fell in love with fish when I was around seven years old, going out fishing for *callig* (pollack) in a little fibreglass boat that my father would row across Port Erin Bay and out around Bradda Head. Pollack are related to cod and haddock and, while they may seem like one of those boring white fish that we seem to love too much in the British Isles, they are actually quite beautiful. They have a deep russet iridescence that varies from fish to fish. Some can look quite dull and brown and others look like they've been wrought from copper sheet. The young ones are often slim and can look spotted or striped, depending on the light. I once saw an enormous shoal of juvenile *callig* as I snorkelled in Spaldrick Bay in early September.

Most of them were smaller than my hand, and while I've usually seen young *callig* of this size lurking in the seaweed in the shallows, these were right out in the water column near the surface in about three metres of water. They were feeding on plankton, darting and nipping and getting very close to me and doing that wonderful curious fish thing, stopping for a moment and looking straight at me. It was magical to interact with these creatures. The more I looked, the more I could see. There were hundreds of these fish, all around the same size, around me in the water in all directions as far as I could see, and the shoal seemed to extend far out into the wider expanse of Port Erin Bay. Shafts of autumn sunlight illuminated the semi-translucent bodies of the young fish. While adult pollack can look quite dull or can be a rich bronzy colour, these youngsters were almost tropical in coloration. They had bright yellow stripes, underlaid with orangey bronze, and their eyes, as they surveyed me, were bright. I hung in the water for about twenty minutes, barely moving and just watching them feed.

The mature *callig* can be quite impressive too and we used to catch some big specimens when I went fishing with my dad as a child. The old Manx people love *callig*. It was the favourite fish of my grandmother, who ate fish every day when she could. She would always extol its superiority to cod. The flesh has a slightly transparent quality, not as matt white as cod. It tastes somehow more fishy – I like it better too.

While *callig* could be relied on as a daily catch, mackerel were more seasonal. Though a really common fish in the British Isles, mackerel are better known for their beauty:

oceanic blue, banded with black, with a shimmering wash of rainbow. Though I haven't fished for years and I don't think that I could now, the sight of a multi-hooked line coming up with six or seven mackerel glinting against a blue sky gives me that hunter's sense of elation, just in recollection.

Mackerel have generally been regarded as a good fish to eat, if they come from well-managed stocks. They have the perfect 'live fast, die young' lifestyle of fish that are usually a sustainable option if they come from a good fishery. They mature at around three years old and produce millions of eggs every year. They grow quickly to marketable size and should be impossible to overfish. When caught in small numbers by inshore boats using lines, they are a great sustainable choice. However, the stocks of mackerel have been in major decline for many years and are caught mainly by a few big companies, who own much of the quota allocated for this species. The majority of mackerel are not caught by small-scale fishermen by line, but by huge factory ships with big seine nets, by the tonne. Year after year, the International Centre for the Exploration of the Seas (ICES) has recommended a sustainable target and the governments of the countries which fish for mackerel have ignored this, exacerbating the downward trend. Advice changes, but some stocks are currently recommended as sustainable by the Marine Conservation Society's excellent *Good Fish Guide* (at the time of writing, line-caught mackerel from Cornwall, for example), while others should be avoided.

Mackerel have beige-coloured meaty flesh, and if you can catch them and eat them on the same day, they really are heaven. They are richly flavoured and don't need to be cooked with much more than oil and a bit of salt and pepper.

Mackerel and *callig* were the species I caught most as a child, so they were the ones I dissected and studied the most growing up. There were other fascinating species of fish around though, and I learnt about some of them in unusual ways.

When I was about four years old my mum had an old-fashioned brown mummy-purse, with one of those snap catches. I wasn't really supposed to go in it but I clearly remember once going into her handbag, finding her purse and getting everything out of it. She had the usual money, stamps, old tickets and receipts, and then in a little zipped pocket she had a strange knobbly little bone-like thing. At the time I think she just told me it was good luck, it came from the Isle of Man and not to root through her purse again. Later, my dad told me more about this strange object – he called it a bollan cross, but it is also known by its Manx Gaelic name, the *crosh vollan*. It is the pharyngeal plate (the grinding bone at the back of the throat/upper palate) of the ballan wrasse.

The wrasse family are known for their ability to clean other fish of predators such as sea-lice, and there are species of wrasse known specifically as cleaner fish. The UK species of wrasse are surprisingly exotic-looking fish, and tropical wrasse are some of the most colourful fish in the ocean. Wrasse, like parrotfish, change sex, starting off as females and becoming males. The mature ballan wrasse is an orangey-brown with green spotty squiggles and a quirky pout. It eats small invertebrates like crabs and shrimps and grinds these up on the pharyngeal plate, studded with small smooth hemispheres of bone. This is what my mum had in her purse, about the size of a 10p.

As a child I just knew they were for good luck, but I've since found out more about what the old fishermen believed about them. They would carry them routinely, as did the Manx mariners who crewed ships sailing throughout the world's oceans, much valued charms to keep them safe on the sea and to protect them from drowning or losing their way. My favourite property of the *crosh vollan* is the reported ability to prevent you making wrong decisions, which sounds very useful.

This superstition is very much still alive in the Isle of Man. Fewer people now seem to carry them around but they have become more popular as charms on necklaces and bracelets and you can even get *crosh vollan* earrings. As I write I reach up to feel for the familiar silver *crosh vollan* I wear most of the time, at the moment strung on a chain with a silver hammerhead shark from the Indian Ocean island of Réunion. A good combination of my marine interests, both global and closer to home.

Ballan wrasse are a great fish to spot when snorkelling around the Isle of Man. You can see quite large specimens darting between clumps of kelp. But they are now part of their own conservation challenge elsewhere. Along with other wrasse species, they are caught live to place in salmon cages to eat their parasites. While this has had serious impacts on their numbers in the wild, there have recently been developments in rearing them in captivity which will hopefully take the pressure off wild stocks and leave this striking fish to the divers and underwater photographers.

*

The newfound use of ballan wrasse is just one example of the urgent need for conservation and good marine management. While they are still inspiring and diverse in places, the seas around the British Isles have been degraded and over-exploited over decades, but unfortunately there are not many people who understand the extent to which this has happened. We are now very used to there being no large rays or oyster banks off the Isle of Man. Our shifting baselines mean we don't appreciate the drastic changes that have happened to marine life over several lifetimes. In the Isle of Man our fisheries today seem relatively healthy, but in a historical context they have completely changed from those of a generation or two ago. In part this is because of politics and administration – we don't have a Manx herring fleet because our fishermen don't have the right paperwork, not because there are no herring to catch. But in part it is to do with the way we and our neighbours have changed the Irish Sea ecosystems. While overfishing of some of the more popular food fishes like cod and herring has been addressed to some extent, the impacts of trawling and dredging on the habitats that sustain these species, and the influence of increasing sea temperatures, have conspired to limit their recovery.

On the wall of my grandmother's old house, which my parents have run as a holiday cottage for more than fifteen years, there is a series of sepia photos that capture a little of the history of the house, and of the Island. In one picture a young girl with long curls and a pinafore dress (looking like she's straight out of an E. Nesbit book) sits on the edge of a large rowing boat. The boat is full of overdressed-looking Victorians – the women wearing elaborate hats and those big cumbersome dresses, the men fully suited. There are some dark-faced, dark-clothed fishermen looking serious at each end of the boat. These are my great-great-grandfather, my great-grandfather and his brothers and the little girl is Katie, my grandmother's aunt. They spent the summer hiring rowing boats and using larger boats to take the wealthier parties of visitors on trips around the bay. Another photo shows the cottage after a rare fall of snow, with people up at the level of the first-floor windows digging down. There is the official wedding photograph of my grandad and grandma. No flouncy white dresses for 1930s Manx brides – they had to be practically dressed in a blouse and skirt to get straight on the ferry for a weekend honeymoon in Liverpool or the Lake District.

My great-great-grandfather, my great-grandfather and my great-great-aunt Katie with a boatload of summer visitors.

One photo always sticks in my mind. It is taken on the far side of Port Erin Bay looking back towards Spaldrick and in the middle of the frame an enormous skate appears to smile for the camera. There is something uncannily human about their large mouths on their undersides. The body of this skate, excluding its tail, is as tall as a person. Strung up on a hook and with its wings extended, angel-like, on both sides it is wider than three men.

There are three leathery-faced fishermen in dark ganseys and matching trousers, a young lad and a man with a moustache wearing a tie, a waistcoat and a light-coloured suit. Under his arm it looks like he is carrying a mac of some sort and he is looking slightly beyond the camera as if watching out for his lift to escape.

This man, so my grandma always said, was a Greek currant merchant based in Liverpool who was a regular visitor to the Isle of Man, chiefly for the game fishing. My grandma, working in her father's chandlery and fishing supplies shop in the front room of their seaside cottage near the main beach in Port Erin, had sold him the tackle that had caught this prize animal and he had given her the photo as a memento. My grandma enjoyed recounting the story, the exotic credentials of the angler, the sheer size of the skate, her own small role in the adventure. As a child it had seemed just that to me, an adventure, but now through the eyes of a marine conservationist, the photo tells a different story.

The giant skate with the men who caught it and Port Erin
Bay in the background.

Skate are cartilaginous fish like sharks, meaning they don't
have a bony skeleton like us, they have a softer structure of
cartilage. The reproductive biology of most skate and rays
makes them very vulnerable. Skate lay small numbers of
eggs, maybe just forty per year, and they can take well over
a year to gestate and release juvenile skate. The mermaid's
purses that we are familiar with (the slim translucent golden
egg cases of spotted catsharks, the current common name
for what you might know better as dogfish) can take five
months or more to hatch, depending on sea temperature.
If a baby skate does make it to adulthood (and as they are
around 15cm across they can easily get caught in trawls
from birth), it will need to survive until it is ten or eleven
years old before it can reproduce itself. With the risk of
capture, and the increasing impacts on their feeding and
breeding habitats, the chances of them getting the chance
to breed are vanishingly small.

As the name suggests, the common skate was once the skate species most often caught in the Irish Sea and beyond. In 1902 marine biologists William Herdman and Robert Dawson, who were working at the Port Erin Marine Laboratory, wrote that the common skate was 'abundant in all parts [of the Irish Sea], and taken by line and by trawling all year round on nearly all our fishing grounds'.

In the 1963 *Marine Fauna of the Isle of Man* authors John Bruce, John Colman and Norman Jones record that the common skate is 'not uncommon in trawl catches'. But in the early 1980s it was reported that over the previous ten years, not a single specimen was caught in over 800 trawls carried out by research vessels in the Irish Sea. In 1940 it accounted for 40 per cent of all skate caught. By 1970 this had declined to 10 per cent and now it is never caught.

This is just one example of how we have lost some of our largest and most charismatic marine species, and because we can't see them and we haven't listened properly to the stories of our grandparents and to the scientists who have tracked these declines, we're not even sad about it. This is the terrible tragedy of shifting baselines and global biodiversity loss, as species after species takes its own route, each different but each heartbreakingly familiar, towards extinction.

The more species we lose, the greater our disconnect with the sea. One important role that fish play culturally is in strengthening that connection. While the number of commercial fishermen, those who make their living from the sea, is now very small compared to in the height of the herring season, many more people use the sea in other ways. Spending time out on a boat or standing on the rocks waiting for a bite on your line can mean that you spot harbour porpoises, puffins or other marine wildlife. The long-standing relationship that we've had with fishing, particularly on the Isle of Man, is reflected in the continued use of Manx names for certain fish, most notably the *callig* (pollack), and to a lesser extent the dogfish (now renamed the lesser spotted catshark) which is known as the *gobbag* and the herring, called *skeddan*.

Manx Gaelic is in the group of Q-Celtic or Goidelic languages, along with Irish and Scottish. Fluent speakers of any of these languages can get by to some extent in the others, although they look very different written down. Manx is written phonetically whereas Irish has a longer tradition of being written and is much less easy to decipher. The Breton language, still widely spoken in Brittany, is in the P-Celtic or Brythonic group with Welsh, still spoken by tens of thousands of people in Wales, and Cornish, which has undergone a revival too.

The revival of the Manx language has been a real success story but it could easily have died out completely. The use of Manx dwindled in the twentieth century and the last native speaker of Manx, Ned Maddrell, died in 1974, though the language had been falling out of use long before that. My grandma was of the generation discouraged from speaking Manx. She didn't learn much as a child and by the 1920s, she remembered her parents speaking it only when they wanted to keep something from the children. But her father would have grown up speaking it as his first language. Fortunately, work to preserve and more importantly use the Manx language predated 1974 so Manx never fell entirely out of use, and now thanks to a concerted revival effort that began in earnest following Ned Maddrell's death, there are now thought to be well over 2000 speakers, including some for whom it is a first language, spoken at home. A recent report concluded that Manx now has a stronger position in the community than it has had for more than a century.

While I love the language and I see it as a vitally important part of my culture and heritage, I am a little ashamed to admit that I am not a Manx speaker, although I have started to learn so many times over the years. My dad took up Manx in his thirties and used to give me informal lessons as he was learning himself when I was still at school. We would listen to crackly cassettes of elderly native speakers in the 1940s greeting each other in wavery voices that at the time I made fun of but now I realise how important these conversations and recordings were to preserve the language and bring it back from the brink. Since then I've gone to evening classes in a church hall in Ballabeg, at the further education college and at the Manx language society in St John's. I even organised a lunchtime Manx class at the Department of the Environment when I was working there but never managed to attend regularly. Some of my former colleagues are really good speakers now. While my own attempts to learn Manx have been a dismal failure I would defend the language to the hilt and I do see its fate intertwined with the fate of the Manx environment. Culture, heritage, language and environment are inextricably linked.

There is some memorable Manx sea vocabulary. The names for jellyfish include *smug raun*, which means seal snot, and *skeeah ny muc varrey*, which literally translates as vomit of the sea pig, the sea pig being the term for porpoise. The critically endangered angelshark, which hasn't been seen in Manx waters for many years and is seen very occasionally elsewhere in the Irish Sea, is known as the *guiy marrey*, the sea goose. A project in Wales is aiming to conserve this amazing species of shark and restore populations in the Irish Sea. It can grow to over two metres in length and is flat-bodied like a ray and camouflaged with tendrils that look like seaweed, allowing it to ambush its prey from the seafloor.

I can't remember when I first started dipping into Fargher's English–Manx dictionary (compiled by Manx scholar Douglas Fargher and published in 1979), but as soon as I did I was hooked. I love language and I love the sea, and Fargher's dictionary is full of the most glorious maritime vocabulary.

For example, the sea-related words are spread over five pages, starting with sea (an entry that takes up a quarter of the page) and ending with sea wrasse (the Manx is *kereyder*). Those pages of Manx sea words tell us so much about the Manx connection with the sea and what was important enough for our ancestors to name specifically and for the brilliant Doug Fargher to warrant inclusion is his remarkable work of scholarship.

There are so many different words for sea – *keayin, mooir, marrey, faarkey* – all used in slightly different ways, as well as the different forms of the words. A mermaid is a *ben varrey* or *mraane marrey*, which both mean sea woman, and Fargher also supplies a nickname for mermaids – *Jonee Ghorrym* (Blue Judith), which is expanded on in A. W. Moore's

A Vocabulary of the Anglo-Manx Dialect as also being a term for seafoam: 'The win' is blawin and *Jonee-ghorryn* is movin.'

Further entries under 'sea' are like a wonderful list of creative writing prompts:

On the high sea – *Er yn ard cheayn*
The whole fleet is at sea – *Ta'n slane flod er y cheayn*
I am still at sea – *Ta me ooilley fud y cheilley*
The spell of the sea – *Druiaght ny marrey*
To follow the sea – *Dy gholl gys yn aarkey*

There is vocabulary for common species and for those rarely seen. For example, the Manx for sea cucumber is *cucowr marrey* but sea cucumbers are quite a rare find in Manx waters. The gravel sea cucumber is one of the many marine animals that can resemble plants – it is a burrowing species with only its mouth tentacles visible, resembling a soft coral or a pale, branched seaweed. Edward Forbes included some beautiful illustrations of sea cucumbers in his 1841 book *A History of British Starfishes*, including one of a chubby sea cherub driving a chariot pulled by sea cucumbers.

The sea lamprey is *creayll*. Sea lampreys are the eel-like primitive fish that latch onto basking sharks with their sucker-like mouths. They can be found detached and living independently (temporarily) in Manx rivers, but again they are a relatively uncommon sighting. There are Manx names for species that are never seen in Manx waters, which will be testimony to the generation of Manx mariners who travelled the world. And there are Manx words for species which may have occurred in Manx waters historically, but are no longer seen. For example, the sea otter is *dooarchoo marrey* (which translates literally as sea beaver). There are no recent records of sea otters in Manx waters or on our shores, although a number of very credible sightings have been reported over the years. A single dead specimen was washed ashore in 2016, but this almost certainly came from a population elsewhere in the Irish Sea.

Then there are the Manx words for seal rookery, sea mouse, sea rock lichen, sea slater and sea slug. And this is just the start. It is such a satisfactory dictionary for a biologist. Mr Fargher doesn't just provide us with the word for the edible or blue mussel commonly seen on the shore or embellishing the rusty legs of the Queen's Pier in Ramsey Bay. He gives us edible mussel – *gob doo* (literally black mouth) – and horse mussel – *gob dhone* (brown mouth). The wonderfully evocative summer shark, *sharkagh souree*, or sun shark, *sharkagh greiney*, are the names for the basking shark, most often seen around our shores between May and August, now and presumably in the period over which our language has evolved.

The dragonet, the wonderful bejewelled gold and sapphire fish of rockpools and shallow waters, is the *dragan traie* – the beach dragon. For seagrass (eelgrass) there is a name for the plant – *faiyr astan* (literally eel grass) – and another name for the root – *pinjane*. In the *Vocabulary of the Anglo-Manx Dialect*, A.W. Moore gives the following example for the use of *pinjane*: 'After a storm we used to be findin *pinjane* on the shore and atin it.' This seems to refer to collecting the eelgrass roots on the shore and making them into porridge, which suggests a much wider extent of the eelgrass beds than we see currently. It would take weeks to collect enough seagrass to make a bowl of porridge with its roots at the rate it is tossed up by the tide these days.

The section on herring is particularly fascinating. The Manx name for the fish is *skeddan*. There are phrases for 'at the herring fishery' – *ec y skeddan*; full-grown herring – *skeddan mie* (literally good herring); gut-pock herring – *skeddan gailley* (which refers to the herring with full stomachs that are caught when there is a lot of plankton around); and back herring – *skeddan y vac* (described as caught off Douglas and the south-east of the Island after the end of August and named after the sea-bank *yn bac*). Wonderfully, 'the smell of herrings is called the *smoghan*'.

Then there are entries for herring bone, herring broth, herring ground, herring gull, herring moth, the Herring-Pond (as the Atlantic Ocean *Yn Atlantagh* was known), herring spawn and herring vessel.

And I told you pollack were important to the Manx. There is the general name *callig*, the northern name *keeil-leig*, the immature pollack *gilpin/giare-chutt*, mackerel-sized *skissack* and large mature *gardash*.

While they were once important for food and fishing, we have no remaining oyster reefs (or banks as they were known), in fact even finding a single live oyster has become a rare event. But we have words for oyster – *ooastyr*; and, evocatively, a word for 'abounding in oysters' – *ooastyragh*. Doesn't that one word tell us so much about our past – that we needed a word for an abundance of oysters? Then we have words for oyster breeder, oyster bed, oys-tercatcher (again there is a southern name *bridjeen* and a northern name *garee breck*), oyster knife and oyster shell.

Edward Forbes wrote in his wonderful *Malacologia monensis – Catalogue of the Mollusca Inhabiting the Isle of Man and the Neighbouring Sea*:

> On the north and east coasts plentiful. The oysters on the north coast are extremely large and very coarse, but those on the east coast are esteemed and brought to market. The bank is situated off the village of Laxey.

In the 1800s there was a thriving oyster fishery off Ramsey and fishermen moved to the Island from the UK and the Channel Islands to join it. In the archives of the *Ramsey Courier* (a Manx newspaper that evolved over the years into the *Isle of Man Courier*, which is now the Isle of Man's weekly free newspaper), there is an obituary of William Bradford who had moved to the Island from Shoreham to join the oyster fishery.

There is a great photo from 1910 of Ramsey Market Square, where there is now a car park with some ornamental trees and electric vehicle charging points. A large crowd is pictured surrounding well over a hundred large cod, far bigger than any cod that are seen today. Cod have been a well-known victim of overfishing, loss of their preferred habitats and, critically, climate change. A northern species, as sea temperatures rise they are being pushed further north.

The Manx for cod is *boiddagh*, which is not commonly used now (unlike *callig* or *gobbag*) and another great Manx word is *slink* – the term for an out-of-condition (usually meaning on the thin side) cod.

In terms of Manx language still in wide use, the celebration of Hop tu Naa has managed to hang on to its Manx Gaelic name against all odds. No other Manx tradition has continued with such vigour. Hop tu Naa (from the Manx for 'this is the night') is a highlight of the Manx calendar. It is our equivalent of Halloween but it is so much more than plastic pumpkins and bowls of gaudily wrapped sweets. For my son Dylan, it is up there with Christmas and birthdays in terms of the anticipation and sense of a real occasion.

Hop tu Naa is the most visible remnant of the Celtic calendar in the Isle of Man. While hardcore Celts and pagans remember and celebrate May Day Eve (Belthane), the end of winter (Laa'l Breeshey) and other highlights of the Celtic calendar, very few residents of the Isle of Man could miss the passing of Hop tu Naa. There was a period in the 1980s when I was growing up when we could have lost our special Hop tu Naa to imported orange pumpkins and the Americanised event that Halloween has now become in the UK. But thanks to determined individuals working for organisations like Culture Vannin and Manx National Heritage, it is now once again a strong Manx tradition. Almost every primary school child could sing you a version of the Hop tu Naa song about Jinnie the Witch that is traditionally sung as you visit neighbours with your spookily carved turnip.

In Ramsey I grew up carving a turnip with a scary face and using the top of the turnip where the leaves grow out as a little chimney for the lantern. The song I learnt was more or less:

Hop tu Naa, Hop tu Naa
Jinnie the Witch is in yer house,
Give us a penny, we'll chase her out.
Hop tu Naa, Hop tu Naa.

Repeated a few times, then:

If you're giving us something,
Give us it soon,
For we want to go home by the light of the moon.
Hop tu Naa.

In the 1990s Manx National Heritage, who run the Island's museums and historical sites, began a Hop tu Naa event at Cregneash, a museum of rural Manx life from the beginning of the twentieth century. They have mounds of turnips (known locally as *moots*) and staff drill them out, to save parents and children spending an entire evening scooping away with a dessert spoon. Then children can do the final carving of faces or spooky scenes and decorate the lanterns. There is also the opportunity to learn one of the many versions of the Jinnie the Witch song, the Hop tu Naa dance, one of the best-known Manx folk dances, and some of the many traditions associated with the evening when the veil between living and dead is at its most flimsy.

More recently, Culture Vannin and the Department of Education have developed all sorts of resources and activities with schools to encourage the learning of Hop tu Naa traditions in schools. And now the children who sing door to door often have a few different verses of the Jinnie song. Local businesses generally avoid talking about

Halloween, and there are lots of references to Hop tu Naa and although the infiltration of big orange supermarket pumpkins is inevitable, there is also wide use of turnips and lots of people call them *moots* now.

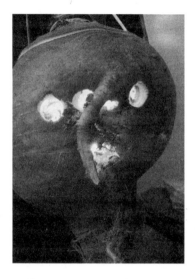

A carved turnip or *moot* for Hop tu Naa.

It makes me so happy that the Manx language is on the ascent. There is a Manx Gaelic primary school in St John's in the centre of the Island, where the children learn exclusively in Manx, which recently celebrated its twentieth anniversary. All other school children have access to Manx lessons from the age of eight and GCSE and A-level Manx is taught in schools. There is an increasing number of families who speak Manx at home, and adults who have grown up in bilingual households. At Tynwald, our ancient outdoor meeting of the Manx parliament which happens every year at St John's on Tynwald Day, 5 July and our national day, the new Manx laws that have been approved that year are read in Manx and English. Manx is very much a living language, and we come across it every day, whether it's in the names of places, in bilingual signage or the remnants of Manx in local dialect. After numerous false starts, I'm afraid my Manx remains basic but I always love to learn a new word, especially if it relates to fish. In contrast, my sister-in-law Ruth Keggin Gell (a wonderful Manx musician and teacher of all things Manx) has recently become *Yn Greinneyder*, a leading role in Manx education that roughly translates as 'the encourager', supporting Manx language learning across the community, and particularly with adult learners. Our language, like our marine life, is our inheritance and we have the opportunity to strengthen and enhance it as we hand it down the generations.

4

Diving In

'Now where Langness runs its long nose into the sea, and on a place now always covered by the waves, there was once a fine city with many towers and gilded domes. Great ships went sailing from its port to all parts of the world, and round it were well-grassed lands with cattle and sheep. Even now sailors sometimes see it through the clear, deep waters, and hear dimly the bleating of sheep, the barking of dogs, and the muffled chiming of bells – "Nane, jees, three, kiare, queig." But no man can walk its streets . . .'

Sophia Morrison, 'The City under the Sea',
Manx Fairy Tales, 1911

Underwater, the sunrise is muted, slowed, as it filters down through thirty metres of plankton-shot sea. As the first rays of light drift down into the viscous darkness of the seabed, waves of larval animals – big-eyed, spindly and almost transparent – begin undulating up through the water column, regaining their daytime positions, finding their place. As it gets lighter, the colours begin to emerge from the dark shapes of the seabed, dotted with bluish phosphorescence. The yellows and oranges of dimpled sponges brighten and the white of the soft corals emerges indistinctly through a blur of tentacles as the individual polyps open to the sun.

Embedded in the sediment, the encrusted shells of horse mussels creak open, displacing fragments of life that are attached to every surface, beginning the constant filtering of seawater for the day. Each shell is separated by millimetres and the whole seabed, disappearing into the living haze, is studded with the orange dashed lines of the hinged openings, underpinning the rippled seabed structure.

As the light touches the seabed, the movement is illuminated and the complex surface heaves and twitches and darts. A cluster of squat lobsters field their waving claws, their papaya-seed eyes flicking to follow their dainty nips of the water column. Dahlia anemones pluck tiny creatures out of passing currents and bronze translucent gobies swim and pause and watch.

Inside their golden purses, embryonic dogfish pulse. A school of pollack emerges from the blue and swims as one creature over a seabed that seems to be jumping up to meet it. And though from time to time a vessel breaks the surface far above, little else disturbs this place. Except, occasionally, the blunt nose of a Risso's dolphin seeking out its prey among the mussels. And rarer still, the gliding bulk of a basking shark looms far above, blocking out the sun so that, momentarily, polyps close and tentacles retract.

A sponge-encrusted spider crab on a horse mussel reef in the
Isle of Man.

I was slowly falling back in love with the Isle of Man.
My new job was going well, and I was spending more
and more time outdoors exploring and rediscovering the
Island. And I had brought a new skill back home with
me – diving. I do regret not having seen more of the Isle
of Man's seascape before I left and went to university. I'd
already been seduced by the gaudy glamour of coral reefs,
but seeing underneath the surface of our surrounding sea
wasn't really on offer when I was growing up. I'd seen
people setting off to go diving, with their inflatable boats
and lots of equipment, but nobody I knew dived or snorkelled. So all my impressions of Manx waters were from
spending a lot of time on the beach, walking on the coast
or going out with my dad in the boat, and spending hours

with my head over the side watching the seabed unfold beneath us.

The first time I dived in Manx waters I'd come back on holiday in between stints working abroad where I'd being doing lots of diving for work. Dad was learning to dive with a local club. He was going out on one of his first boat dives and I asked if I could join them. At that point I hadn't learnt how to dive with a dry suit and had a thick wet suit that I'd used for some of my tropical diving where I was underwater for a long time at shallow depths and would get cold.

That first dive was to a rocky reef area north of Douglas, the capital of the Isle of Man. I had that unfamiliar shock of the cold water on my face and then the strangest experience. The water was perfectly clear and everything I could see looked oddly familiar. Kelp and other seaweed, even the slate rock and the pebbles, and then the lobster someone pointed out in a slaty crevice, the whelks and the king scallops flush with the gravel. All the creatures were familiar and everyday to me but in their dead and desiccated forms, cast up on the shore. To see everything alive and busy and bathed in ten metres of the clearest water for the first time felt odd, to say the least. It was like visiting someone you know well in an unfamiliar house.

That experience was also special because it was the first and only time I'd dived with my dad, the person who'd introduced me to the sea and nurtured my great love of it. Although he has never become a regular diver, I was so pleased that he learnt in the Isle of Man and got the opportunity to see beneath the surface of our wonderful

Manx sea and some of the fish he'd grown up loving too. He was so thrilled to dive in Port Erin Bay, where he's spent so much time on the surface looking down, and the ballan wrasse particularly delighted him.

We had been underwater together before, when my parents visited me in the British Virgin Islands where I first worked as a marine biologist after graduating. We were off the perfect sandy curve of the Long Bay on Beef Island and it was his first ever attempt at snorkelling, with me as a not particularly helpful teacher. Our second trip was to Hans Creek, a magical place where I spent most days underwater and a resident barracuda who sometimes hovered behind me during my work appeared on cue for my dad and he still remembers it. In Hans Creek he was able to see for himself some of the child's drawing tropical fish that I had fallen in love with in the tropics. Bright yellow tangs darting around like purposeful flower petals, grumpy-faced damsels storming to the surface to convey their displeasure at anything that invaded their territory, and meditative trumpet fish camouflaged as a part of the sea surface, their large calm eyes following you as they drifted nearby.

That first dive was special because I saw Manx marine life from a new perspective, and because it was with my dad, but it wasn't really a taste of just how extraordinary our waters are. That would come later, after I moved back to work.

A common starfish.

By 2008 I had been back on the Isle of Man for five years. I was diving fairly regularly but this outing was particularly special. We were sitting either side of the RIB (an inflatable boat), kitted up and getting instructions from Caroline Perry and Phil Roriston who had taken me to see a site they had discovered.

We dropped right on the reef, which stretched out in all directions. I checked my gauge – thirty-six metres – and the water was still, clear and daylit. But when I swept my torch across the scene the colours burst from every surface. There were sponges everywhere. Sponges like tangerines sat alone and a sunflower encrusting sponge grew over a spider crab that only revealed its carefully camouflaged self by moving. The mermaid's purses pulsed with embryonic dogfish caught in amber. Red and robotic, squat lobsters snapped at the air. And everywhere the sunset colours of soft corals, no longer the clammy dead men's fingers of their name, were in full glory, a fur of polyps out and feeding in the current. For the first few minutes I was completely focused on the surface creatures, their busy community clicking and snapping and waving their arms. Then I exhaled fully again, sinking head-first towards the seabed, and saw my first horse mussel – the plain brown-grey bivalve transformed by its coat of encrusting sponges and seaweeds. Its shells were slightly open, filtering the sea. Once I'd got my eye in I could see that every inch beneath the reef was built of these half-buried shells.

This was the horse mussel reef that Caroline and Phil only discovered in 2007, a year before this dive. They'd been carrying out surveys and documenting its extent and photographing the breathtaking diversity of a habitat we might lose completely to climate change in a few decades.

This fragment that I'd finally seen in the briny flesh is old. It must have been here hundreds, if not thousands, of years, building up the seabed in a jumble of dead shell and living creatures. It was like finding a little patch of ancient woodland, giving me a glimpse into historic seas before we trawled and dredged them.

I couldn't stop smiling but too soon I felt the tug of the changing tide. Caroline was clipping her camera on and Phil signalled to ascend. They are diver-explorers who have scoured maps and kept meticulous records to find the most exciting and diverse dive sites in places that most people would never even think of diving. In my delight at the horse mussels I'd forgotten they were there.

Queen scallops and sponges on the Little Ness horse mussel
reef, Isle of Man.

Working as the Isle of Man Government's first marine
conservation officer, I had the opportunity to experience
everything you could imagine involved with protecting
the sea. I examined dead marine animals to work out why
they'd died, recorded the spread of invasive alien species,
I went out on fishing boats to study the catches, surveyed
rockpools for warmer-water species creeping north and
studied our coastal waters and the historic research that
had been done to find important species and habitats that
needed to be protected. I also spent an awful lot of time
sitting at a computer in the office or worse, at endless
meetings as I began to understand the bureaucracy of
government.

I have to be honest – before I did some work on the
Irish Sea while I was a post-doctoral researcher in York, not

long before returning to the Isle of Man, I had no idea of the diversity of Manx marine life and in particular about the incredible variety of temperate reefs. This is a broad classification but encompasses rocky reefs – rocks covered with diverse seaweeds and animal turfs that are home to a wealth of species – and also biogenic reefs, which are reefs where the structure is built by animals (tropical coral reefs are an example) but are amazingly diverse. The most notable example of a biogenic reef in Manx waters is a horse mussel bed, which the mussels can build up the seabed by metres with their own bodies. We also have areas of blue mussel beds on the shore and on the seabed which are home to hundreds of species and important food for birds.

Although few marine experiences rival the richness and colour of a horse mussel reef (in my opinion anyway!), you don't have to dive to discover wonderful, diverse marine communities. Before I began diving around the Isle of Man, I was inspired by the diversity of life on the shore and I still take great delight in rockpooling. If you go on your own, rockpooling can be the ultimate mindfulness experience. If you start right down at the lowest tide mark, there is a wonderful smell of pure sea as the seabed is exposed to the air. Find a rock right by the edge of the water and you can sit quietly and hear little pops and clicks as the seaweed settles, the limpets clamp down onto the rocks and the marine life battens down the hatches for a few hours of intertidal life. Then you can start your search. Underneath an overhang of rock encrusted in sponges and dog whelk eggs you find a lovely little pink cushion star; they really do look like little velvet pin cushions. You admire it, then carefully put it back where you found it. A beautiful butterfish, snake-like and wonderfully marked with black spots, freezes as you lift a rock so you get a few moments to look closely at its sad little face before it slithers into the seaweed. In a calm pool a wine-red beadlet anemone feeds on a passing shrimp and you can watch the whole thing. Sometimes something unexpected has found itself stranded in a larger pool, maybe a lumpfish or a gurnard, both remarkably exotic-looking fish that you wouldn't normally encounter on the shore. A real find might be a tiny nudibranch or sea slug – there are dozens of species in our waters. Unlike our rather dull land slugs, they are covered in feathery projections, little explosions of colour. Each has a slightly different way of laying its eggs in whorls and squiggles to help you identify them and it is often the eggs that you see first.

A king scallop hidden on the seabed in gravel and maerl.

Diving or snorkelling around the British Isles gives you a fabulous insight into our world-class marine life, but both require a certain level of organisation and equipment. For rockpooling, all you need are some wellies or waterproof sandals and a tide table and you're set. You get to see full-blown marine life exposed for a short time at low tides. It is the closest you will get to experiencing seabed life without diving and it's a chance to find species you've never seen before. Looking back to shore from the lowest low-tide mark also gives you a new perspective on the land – a shore crab's view of the world.

One of the unsung aspects of our rocky shores is the diversity of seaweed. A single rockpool may be home to dozens of different species, from the lovely pink encrusting coralline seaweeds that are often splashed around the insides of rockpools like gaudy paint, to the better-known bladder wrack with its big grape-like bubbles to keep the plant afloat at high tide. This natural diversity is at risk from invasive species, in particular a species called wireweed, a pretty Japanese seaweed which has taken hold throughout the British Isles in recent years. In the Isle of Man it was first spotted in 2005 by a colleague of mine and in just a few years had taken hold around the coast. Wireweed is a fine brown seaweed, identified by holding up a strand and watching for the branch-like fronds to fall down at regular intervals like washing hanging on a line. It has little round fruiting bodies which when released distribute the seaweed over large distances. In rockpools the weed tends to float at the surface and form dense mats that can shade out other species. There is some debate about how negative an impact wireweed has, but it is likely that some native algal species are outcompeted as it becomes ubiquitous on our shores. Underwater the seaweed looks fragile and delicate but in some places it has outcompeted native protected eelgrass, leading to further declines in this important species. Another invasive seaweed is the wonderfully named oyster thief which forms shower-cap-shaped puffs of air encased in a khaki seaweed cover. The unusual name comes from the observation that when these air-filled cushions grew on oysters (when oysters and oyster reefs were a common part of our ecosystems in the British Isles), they were able to use their buoyancy to detach the oysters from the seabed completely.

A group organised by the Manx Wildlife Trust rockpooling on Ramsey beach.

The most exciting time to go rockpooling is a low spring tide. This is when creatures that will spend most of their lives fully underwater are temporarily revealed. There is nothing like stepping carefully out over the glistening kelp-covered seabed that emerges in the last minutes before the lowest tide. Look underneath rocks and boulders, and their under-surfaces will be festooned with sponges and sea anemones and every crevice will be inhabited by clusters of baby blue mussels, lemon-yellow dog whelk eggs and pale sea squirts.

My favourite and most familiar beach for this is Spaldrick beach, where I spent long hours rockpooling as a child. We tended to keep to the rockpools further up the beach in my childhood but as an adult I discovered the delights at the lowest ranges of the intertidal habitat. Spaldrick beach is dominated by kelp in the lower reaches of the shore and this extends into the shallow waters of the bay. There is something otherworldly about venturing out through the draped fronds of kelp at low tide. It can initially be difficult to get your head around the idea that just a couple of hours earlier the water in this spot would have been well over the top of your head, and all those lazy drapes of weed lifted high around you into an undulating curtain of glossy brown kelp.

Really low spring tides come around just a few times a year (closest to the equinoxes around 21 March and 21 September) and they vary from year to year, so some areas of seabed may be revealed only every few years. In these lower reaches it is easier to make the most exciting rockpool finds as the creatures are unaccustomed to being exposed. Deep-blue lobsters may still be scuttling for cover, encumbered by claws more than half the length of their body. My favourite low-tide find is always a cushion star. These stout little starfish are often a tasteful pale green or orange, and like to wedge themselves into crevices and take refuge under rocks. Butterfish are another lovely find. With long eel-like bodies and distinctive spots along their flanks, these fish can often be found curled up and stock-still underneath rocks.

Mermaid's purses – spotted catshark egg cases on a horse mussel reef.

Up at the high-tide mark, an exciting discovery on the strandline is a mermaid's purse. These are the egg cases of sharks and rays and have become less common finds around our shores as populations of rays in particular have declined over the past decades. While it is still quite common to find the long caramel-coloured egg cases of dogfish (the small, spotted sandpaper-skinned sharks most commonly seen in our waters and confusingly now known as spotted catshark), the squarer black mermaid's purses of skate and rays are now becoming rare finds. The Shark Trust, a UK charity specialising in shark and ray conservation, runs a very effective citizen science project, 'The Great Eggcase Hunt', encouraging people to report their finds of mermaid's purses and to learn how to identify them. If you're really keen, you can sign up to provide data from timed searches which gives more detailed information about the abundance and distribution of these imperilled species.

I love exploring beaches and I am a big advocate of investigating their treasures to begin to appreciate the wonders of the sea, something everyone can do if they have access to the shore. But there is nothing like diving down to the seabed and seeing habitats that maybe only a few people have ever seen before you. In Manx waters, at a less popular dive site, you may even be the first to see that particular vista underwater.

If I had to choose a favourite marine habitat to dive I would be truly stuck. Tropical coral reefs, with their technicolour glamour and unfeasibly diverse fish populations, are the habitats that sold me on marine ecosystems. On coral reefs so much is on show, you can clearly see the complexity of the habitat created by the coral animals in their different approaches to colonial living. Then tropical seagrass beds seduced me with their hidden diversity and quiet productivity and life-saving abilities to provide food, shelter and trap carbon from the atmosphere in the mud between their roots. In tropical seas, much store is given to the interconnectedness of coral reefs, seagrass meadows and mangroves. Each habitat plays an important role in the life cycle of fish and invertebrates and the movements between these three key habitats is essential for many species. In temperate waters it is my revered trinity of maerl beds, eelgrass meadows and horse mussel reefs that I've come to adore and champion at every opportunity. The linkages between the three is not so clear, but they represent such diversity of structures and functions and I love them. I have a big bag in my office at home with a box of bleached-looking dead maerl, some horse mussel shells and a pressed sample of *Zostera marina* along with photos of all the habitats in Manx waters. I use the contents of this bag less often now, but in my marine conservation officer role I would need the curious contents most weeks as my props for a lecture, stakeholder meeting or a visit to a school.

Mussels have always fascinated me. When I first moved back to the Island, I was really excited to find out about the horse mussel reef in the Ballacash Channel, which local marine biologist Dr Terry Holt had found in the early 1990s. But it can't really have been their beauty that captured me, because the photos from those surveys predate digital cameras so they are a bit blurred and you can't really make much out. Perhaps it was the longevity of the horse mussels that was so captivating. Used to king scallops where a fifteen-year-old is an amazing discovery (particularly because they are fished and mainly caught at just two or three years old), I found a smaller bivalve that could live to fifty years old exciting. Or maybe it was the stories of the Jones Teardrop (as it is known to a small circle of horse mussel enthusiasts), a large drop-shaped area of horse mussel reef to the south-east of the Island. There is not much left of the reef now, but it was once a good source of horse mussels which bivalve expert Dr Andy Brand recalls being collected for the giant barnacles attached to their shells, mysteriously of interest to Liverpool University dental school.

Horse mussels are quite similar in appearance to the edible or blue mussels you may be familiar with, from either eating them or seeing them growing on the shore. They generally tend to be larger – they can grow to about 20cm in length, whereas edible mussels don't tend to get much larger than 10cm and they are usually much smaller than that. Rather than the midnight blue of an edible mussel, a horse mussel is often browner and many are almost black in colour. They are a very common species and can live as single individuals or in small clumps, but it is when they form big interconnected reefs that they become a rare and threatened habitat – the horse mussel reef. A well-known trait of edible mussels is the strong byssus threads that they use to bind to each other and to substrates. In Ramsey Bay on the Isle of Man, the rusting legs of the iron pier are a favourite place to find clumps of edible mussels tightly bound to each other and to the structure of the pier. Horse mussels use their threads to form dense clumps, with many of the mussels half-buried in the sand or gravel underneath. In a dense horse mussel reef there can be over a hundred mussels in a metre square. When you're diving over them or looking at photographs taken from a survey vessel, the best way to identify all these mussels is by looking for the straight pale yellow or orange slits of their slightly open shells.

In the Isle of Man we are spoilt with horse mussel reefs and we have some of the most diverse reef communities in the British Isles. We've undoubtedly lost large areas over the last century since scallop dredging has proliferated, but we have some remarkable reefs that still appear to be thriving and which demonstrate the diversity and resilience of this underrated habitat. The horse mussel reef at Little Ness (where I dived with Caroline and Phil) is like a slightly raised platform of densely packed marine life built on foundations of horse mussels and also shored up with embedded queen scallops and other species of bivalve that add to the complexity of the reef. When scientists Dr Clara Mackenzie and Prof. Bill Sanderson from Heriot-Watt University surveyed the diversity of the horse mussel reef a few years ago they identified 300 species from one small set of samples, and further analysis led by Dr José Fariñas-Franco has revealed more about the biodiversity of this special site. The species include sponges, spider crabs, squat lobsters, sea urchins and starfish, and the work is highlighting the importance of Manx horse mussel reefs on a British Isles scale.

Horse mussel reefs favour some of the most challenging places in our waters. They thrive in areas where they are safe from the wave action of shallower waters but where tidal currents are strong. The horse mussel reef in the Ballacash Channel has tidal currents rushing past it for over twenty-three hours every day. There are just twenty minutes every tidal cycle when the current isn't roaring past.

Horse mussels have some of the classic attributes of species that are vulnerable to human impacts. Unlike many species of bivalve, horse mussels are relatively slow to mature and only begin to reproduce at around five years of age. The larvae they do produce are also very picky and don't settle easily, so a very small proportion of the millions of offspring produced by a spawning horse mussel actually survive. I've only occasionally seen young horse mussels and they are curious creatures – caramel-coloured with long golden hair-like barbs on their shells.

Diving on the horse mussel reefs off the Point of Ayre.

The deep, current-swept nature of horse mussel reefs means that I've rarely had the opportunity to dive on them. When Prof. Sanderson, Dr Rohan Holt, Dr Jo Porter and their team from what was then the Countryside Council for Wales came over to explore the horse mussel reefs of the Ballacash Channel, the challenging technical diving involved was beyond my capability and I stayed on the boat. My job was supporting the divers with the shore-side preparations including letting the shipping companies (whose vessels steam up and down the channel every day between Wales and Ireland) know that we were going to have divers in the water on their route. Those reefs are formed into high mounds, reaching as much as two metres from the sandy seabed. The horse mussels themselves are half-buried in the seabed and barely visible and what you really notice are the white and orange blooms of the soft coral *Alcyonium digitatum* (dead men's fingers). The mussels and the soft corals love the streaming current running past them because they are both feeding on passing plankton. Each hand-like protrusion of soft coral is made up of thousands of individual coral polyps which extend their tentacles into the tide to catch plankton. The horse mussels also catch living plankton and other bits of organic matter, filtering it out of the passing water.

The diversity of horse mussel reefs captivates me, especially because I had no idea such a rich habitat even existed for the first thirty years of my life. But their utility is also astonishing. Horse mussel reefs cover large areas, perhaps hundreds of square metres in at least five major sites in Manx waters that we have confirmed, and undoubtedly many more. Their filtering of seawater on that scale becomes a really important function in keeping our waters clear and clean. Those low platforms or high mounds are also stabilising the sandy and gravelly sediment they grow on, providing stable homes and places to attach for the hundreds of species that live among the mussels and those that need a hard surface to cling to as they make the transition from plankton to benthos (bottom-dwelling). Biogenic reefs like horse mussel reefs and oyster reefs are finally getting a bit more attention internationally as the initiatives to protect and restore them become more widespread, and they are valued as part of a wider ocean rewilding movement.

A view of the horse mussel reef in the Ballacash Channel with soft corals growing on the mussels.

Another favourite habitat that is beginning to get more international attention, to my delight, is maerl. My enchantment with maerl came on gradually. Not long after I'd started my role as marine conservation officer, an ex-Port Erin Marine Laboratory marine biologist now working in IT got in touch to say he had some marine survey data that might be useful. Dr Lewis Veale told me about the dive surveys he'd been involved in around the Island in the 1990s. Part of the work was a really detailed survey of sites in Ramsey Bay, highlighting high concentrations of live maerl, horse mussels and edible mussels. He handed over a wealth of data in spreadsheets and hundreds of photos. The photos were colourful, good quality and some of the most striking showed bubblegum-pink maerl studded with different species of anemones. It was very exciting.

What is maerl? I must have found pieces of it when I was beachcombing as a child. We probably thought it was coral, and 'corals' is the name it is commonly known as by Manx fishermen. On the beach it resembles little white branching trees of calcium carbonate (our bones are made of something similar) which can range from tiny fragments smaller than your fingernail to more substantial structures as big as the palm of your hand. You can find them on many beaches around the Isle of Man, but I've always found Ramsey beach and the shore stretching north to the Point of Ayre the best place to see it.

A nodule of maerl about 5cm across and
bright pink in colour.

Because of the coral-like structure, it is easy to mistake maerl for coral or some other colonial animal. But this unlikely organism is in fact a type of red seaweed, a coralline algae – a seaweed with a hard structure. Living maerl glows pink because over that delicate white calcium carbonate skeleton is a very thin layer of the living pink seaweed. The seaweed uses the light that filters down from the surface to photosynthesise and slowly lay down layer upon layer of calcium carbonate, allowing the nodule to grow by around a millimetre per year. So even the tiniest of nodules represents a good few years' growth. To create a maerl bed, centuries' worth of nodules may have accumulated in one place, with just those nodules on the surface flushed pink and still living.

If you haven't seen those little coral fragments, you will have seen pink encrusting coralline algae in rockpools or in shallow water. Sometimes the pink can be so vivid and in such contrast to the surrounding dark grey slate that it can look like someone has spilt paint. It can completely encrust pebbles so they look like they're made of a rare and strange pink mineral. Once when I was out collecting samples on a survey at sea, I found a curiously man-made-looking rectangle completely encrusted in pink maerl, as if dipped in paint that has been in the shed too long. It looked like someone's credit card had sat on the seabed and been colonised but when, consumed with curiosity, I broke off a little corner, it was a strange thin slate of a sandstone-like material. Beautiful and unusual, I keep it in my desk drawer like a talisman.

Maerl provides the perfect home for marine creatures. The branching nodules interlink into a complex mesh with lots of little spaces in between. During the surveys of maerl in Ramsey Bay, Lewis and his colleagues found hundreds of species, from spider crabs that look like they've been assembled from spare legs in a game of Beetle, to the blood-red blooms of dahlia anemones, some pure red, others streaked in white and pink, reminiscent of their namesake at horticultural shows.

I have spent so much time talking about maerl. For many years I ran a marine conservation evening class and I now do occasional lectures and workshops and for those I have a big plastic tub of dead white maerl skeletons that I use not only to show people maerl, but also for an exercise to think about why it is such a special and important habitat. People can pick up handfuls of it, like rummaging through Lego, and think about what lives between the pieces when it's submerged and topped with the pink icing of live maerl. For a long time most people hadn't heard of it, but through education and conservation work it is becoming better known in the Isle of Man and across the British Isles. One of the examples I gave in my teaching of impacts on this species habitat was the dredging of maerl to be used as agricultural fertiliser. The perfectly sized little nodules make a very convenient way to apply calcium carbonate (lime) to agricultural land. Fortunately though, maerl is much more valued now as a marine habitat and this practice is no longer such a threat.

What makes maerl so magical? The colour is other-worldly. In the same way that a diver new to the underwater life of the British Isles can't quite believe the vivid green of a lush eelgrass meadow, so when you first see a rich, deep patch of living maerl it is difficult to believe that this almost fluorescent pink is natural. And the enamelled filigree of maerl is studded with other colours. So many different species of anemones are embedded within; tiny painted crabs, sponge-encrusted and seeming to move almost as slowly as the maerl grows; the deep red of the wonderfully named bloody Henry starfish.

The more you learn about maerl, the more captivating it becomes. At a workshop for fishermen in 2004 at Millport Marine Laboratory on the island of Little Cumbrae in the Clyde (sadly also now closed as a research laboratory), marine biologist and leading maerl expert Dr Nick Kamenos from the University of Glasgow had set up a demonstration of an experiment he had been doing. He had tanks with living pink rosy maerl on one side and then pale dead maerl and gravel on the other side. He would place dozens of juvenile queen scallops, like babies' fingernails, in the tanks and leave them overnight. Almost without exception, the queen scallops would flitter and flap over into the living maerl side of the tank, clearly preferring this habitat. Researchers have also found that cod prefer healthy maerl beds as foraging grounds and the densities of scallops, starfish and other species are higher in healthy maerl. Living maerl provides a structurally complex habitat within which a vulnerable young bivalve can wedge itself and be relatively safe and sheltered from predators. Studies by Dr Jason Hall-Spencer, also working at the Millport Marine Laboratory at the time, have revealed over 500 species of marine animal and 150 species of seaweed associated with the maerl beds there.

Maerl is found all over the world but it does seem to have strong Celtic connections. Not only is it found in

Wales, Ireland, Scotland and the Isle of Man, but it has also been well studied in the Fal Estuary in Cornwall. The name maërl (also written maërl) originates from a Celtic language, Breton (which is in the P-Celtic or Brythonic group along with Cornish and Welsh), and the habitat is also common and well studied around Brittany. In North America and internationally maerl is better known as rhodolith beds (from the Greek for red rocks) and is found extensively from the poles to the equator. I first encountered living rhodolith beds in the seagrass meadows of Quirimba Island in Mozambique when I was surveying the fishing grounds to understand the ecology that supported the fisheries there. There is an enormous rhodolith bed on the Abrolhos Shelf in Brazilian waters which has been compared to the Great Barrier Reef in its extent and ecological importance, and researchers and conservationists are working hard to raise the profile of this lesser-known and therefore less-protected habitat.

Perhaps because it is still so little known, maerl has seen declines throughout its range. From the Arctic Circle to the Algarve, fishing, marine developments and pollution have been eroding away once extensive beds of living maerl. And these beds have an amazing history. Each little nodule of maerl, the size of a dried apricot, can be up to fifty years old and they grow unimaginably slowly. In Iona, Scotland, nodules of maerl found at the bottom of the bed were found to be 4000 years old, and in some places the maerl beds are thought to date back to the end of the last ice age (over 8000 years). The easily disturbed nature of the loosely associated beds, the incredibly slow growth and the lack of appreciation of the importance of this blancmange pink habitat mean that it is really vulnerable to destruction and also very difficult to restore once it is lost. It is also at increasing risk from climate change. A recent study predicted that climate change could mean that maerl is reduced by as much as 85 per cent by the end of this century.

The maerl in Ramsey Bay is not particularly deep, but it is extensive. In some places there is a high proportion of living maerl (a good indication of health), with numerous species happily nestled in its sheltering crannies and crevices. The best-quality maerl I've seen around the Island has been in small patches, protected on all sides by rocks and presumably therefore never impacted by dredging and trawling. Given natural protection for centuries, these little patches yielded much bigger nodules than I'd seen before in deeper pinks and in between them some of the largest scallops I've ever seen. These giant scallops produce exponentially more juveniles than smaller animals so the presence of a relatively small number of these super scallops in their luxury maerl homes plays a really important role in sustaining the scallop fishery.

The Island holds other secrets. Langness peninsula juts out from the Isle of Man like a foot beneath a perching bird. It is an Area of Special Scientific Interest, a popular stopping-off point for many migrating birds including Brent geese and curlew, and the only location in the British Isles where you can find the lesser mottled grasshopper. Across a narrow causeway from the peninsula you can walk across to an islet known as Fort Island where Derby Fort, a well-preserved round fort, dates back to the time of the

English Civil War. Nearby, the ancient *keeill* (the Manx term for the small, ancient chapels that dot the landscape) is older still, on a site that is nearly 1000 years old. Tides rip around the peninsula in a chop of messy sea, and the waters are the perfect place to spot Risso's dolphins. These white, blunt-headed cetaceans can grow to four metres in length and are usually seen further offshore, but around the Isle of Man they often feed close in and can be spotted leaping clear out of the water. Risso's dolphins' favourite food is squid and elsewhere they are known to feed around horse mussel reefs and other habitats that encourage squid and other cephalopods.

In the inlet between the peninsula and Fort Island there is a narrow inlet facing out into the Irish Sea. I'd often seen it as I'd crossed over the causeway to Fort Island but I had never realised the gulley had an exciting secret. Not long after I moved back to the Isle of Man, I met Steve, an old friend and keen diver who told me there was an eelgrass bed in the inlet at Langness and offered to take me diving to see it. It was a shore dive – we got into our drysuits and put on our dive kit in the car park on Fort Island and then slipped and slithered over the weed-covered rocks into water dark with knotted wrack and kelp. The swim out took us from submerged rocky shore, with familiar seaweeds and the occasional limpet, down into a startling emerald city of eelgrass. In just five metres of clear, sunlit water, the eelgrass was the brightest green which seemed to reflect off everything else, so even the rocks and the brown seaweeds had a greenish hue. I had expected something murkier, more patchy, and now I was smiling into my regulator at the splendour of

homegrown Manx eelgrass. I had travelled over 8000 kilometres to study Mozambican seagrass and this had been on
my doorstep. Steve pointed out a large mauve snakelocks
anemone attached to an eelgrass stem, waving in the slight
swell like a fistful of pale worms. Clouds of rust-coloured
two-spot gobies drifted over the meadow and as I exhaled
and sank down into the seagrass understorey, I spotted a
cold metallic eye looking up at me. A slim fish a handspan
in length peeked out from between the stems, a curious
fifteen-spined stickleback. As we stumbled and slid back
up the shore to the car park I couldn't stop talking about
the dive. Steve had been visiting the site for a few years
and knew it well. He told me how the eelgrass had been
spreading slowly each year and now almost completely
filled the little underwater gulley.

Seagrasses are flowering plants that grow underwater
and on the shore, from the tropics to the cool waters of
the Arctic. They can form vast meadows extending over
hundreds of kilometres, and are confined to shallow coastal
waters where they are able to photosynthesise. They have
high ecological value, providing nursery areas for many
species of fish and invertebrates and also stabilising sandy
seabeds and making habitats suitable for many species.

The captivating seagrass off Langness is eelgrass, *Zostera
marina*, one of only two seagrass species commonly found
in the British Isles. Eelgrass is a tall slim species of seagrass,
quite similar to the tropical *Enhalus acoroides* (tape seagrass)
which I studied for my PhD, but finer. It grows underwater, commonly at between five and ten metres' depth
where there is still plenty of sunlight for photosynthesis.
And it is also known occasionally to grow on the shore

below the high-water mark, drying out at low tide and then resubmerging. Another species, dwarf seagrass (*Zostera noltei*), is more common on the shore and is an important food for geese and other birds, but this species hasn't yet been recorded in the Isle of Man.

Before it closed, the Port Erin Marine Laboratory library looked out across an exposed and unpredictable stretch of water to Milner's Tower and the jagged profile of Bradda Head with its nineteenth-century mine workings and streaks of green from the copper ore; the best library view I had ever seen. The library had a wonderful collection of books and reports collected over the long history of the lab. Doing some research for a lecture I was writing one day, I was excited to find a map of the bay in a report from 1919 with areas of eelgrass clearly marked as *Zostera*. That started my mission to find eelgrass in Port Erin Bay. I was living in Port Erin at the time, just above Spaldrick beach where I would sometimes swim before work. Other times I'd put on my mask and snorkel and swim out along the far side of the bay where the *Zostera* was marked on the map. I spent many hours looking for eelgrass in the bay, both by snorkelling and whenever I got a chance to dive in the bay. I wasn't the only one keen to track the elusive habitat down.

For many years Tony Glen ran the local branch of Seasearch, an initiative led by the Marine Conservation Society in the UK which trains recreational divers to carry out survey dives that can contribute to marine science and management. Tony is a fellow seagrass enthusiast and he too had been searching Port Erin Bay for eelgrass, to no avail. Port Erin Bay is a popular dive-training site, so Tony and his diving friends were often in the water there. He has also dived at other locations in the bay, hoping to find it. If we hadn't seen the historic records for eelgrass in that report, we might not have expected to find seagrass in Port Erin Bay. The bay faces south-west, right into the prevailing winds, and is certainly not the typical sheltered location you'd normally find eelgrass. I know from personal experience the force of the storms that can roar into the bay in the winter and it does seem surprising that seagrass could ever have established and thrived there. However, a bit of local history may explain this. In 1876, when Port Erin was thriving as a tourist destination, a breakwater was built halfway across the mouth of the bay in an attempt to protect the harbour from the prevailing wind. The construction of the breakwater was one of the biggest engineering projects undertaken in the Isle of Man and it was expensive and challenging. After thirteen years under construction, the breakwater lasted only five years before it was destroyed in a winter storm in 1881. But those few years of shelter may have been enough for the eelgrass to establish and hang on for a few decades.

We had more luck in the north of the Island though. When I was gathering information on Manx marine habitats, I spoke to a retired fisherman who phoned the office one day after seeing an article in the local paper. He told me he had seen eelgrass in Ramsey Bay over sixty years earlier. He described how he made himself a viewing device – replacing the bottom of a bucket with a piece of glass – so he could easily see the seabed in clear, shallow waters to help him place his crab and lobster pots in the right place. Following up on this tip, we searched the area, diving and snorkelling whenever we got the opportunity. Eventually on a grey autumn day and fighting an unexpectedly strong current in what looked like a sheltered corner of Ramsey Bay, we found our first patch of eelgrass, very close to where the ex-fisherman had suggested. This is a good example of how it is often fishermen who know our sea best and can help conserve it.

Until very recently, seagrass beds have languished in the shadow of their more glamorous and internationally known neighbours, coral reefs. But I'm pleased to report that, as I write, they are having their moment in the limelight, which is wonderful. While coral reefs are now often highlighted as the global habitat at most immediate risk from climate change, seagrass beds may well be part of the solution. The *Blue Planet II* BBC TV series highlighted the value of mangroves, seaweeds and seagrasses globally and brought the concept of blue carbon to a wider audience. Blue carbon is defined as the carbon captured by the world's ocean and coastal systems. Many marine habitats are able to take carbon dioxide out of the atmosphere and lock it down, reducing the impact of global climate change. Three main habitats have been identified as the blue carbon superheroes – mangroves, seagrasses and saltmarshes store a large proportion of the global carbon trapped in marine sediments.

Seagrasses have seen a huge decline in recent years, as a result of damaging fishing methods, pollution, coastal development and other impacts. By recent estimates we may be losing as much as 7 per cent of seagrass habitat every year. Seagrass restoration has long been practised in some parts of the world, so the techniques are out there. Large-scale initiatives to restore this essential habitat have been slow to develop but are now accelerating around the world as the vital role of seagrass is recognised.

A lobster in an eelgrass meadow, Ramsey Bay, Isle of Man.

What difference could seagrass conservation and restoration make to emissions? It has recently been estimated that global carbon emissions may be increased by between 3 and 19 per cent by the loss of coastal vegetation. The contribution to emissions made by the loss of seagrasses has been estimated at around 10 per cent of the emissions from land-use change. Current global initiatives, just beginning to take off, to restore seagrass beds to their pre-industrialisation extent could make a significant contribution to the carbon stored in marine sediments and to the extent of climate change. Studies have shown that if seagrasses are restored, their capacity to store carbon can increase year on year for eighteen years or more.

A message which is also just beginning to take hold, and which came clearly out of the United Nations Framework Convention on Climate Change Conference of Parties (COP26) in Glasgow in November 2021, is that before we even think of restoration we must effectively protect the carbon-storing habitats we already have. As with any habitat, it is much easier and cheaper to maintain existing seagrass beds than to restore a complex habitat, so the use of marine protected areas and other measures to guard existing habitats with high carbon storage capacity should be a global priority (and many countries are now committing to protecting 30 per cent of their seas by 2030). And in view of the alarming decline in seagrass around the world, year on year, reversing this decline with active seagrass habitat restoration will be essential.

There are increasing opportunities for seagrass and other blue carbon projects to be funded by carbon financing schemes (investing in projects that help tackle climate change), and this needs to be embraced internationally. It is really heartening to see that in the last few years, seagrass has become the popular face of blue carbon and people are talking more and more about how managing the sea more effectively and taking care of ocean life can provide solutions for climate change. Dynamic charity Project Seagrass has played an important role in promoting seagrass in the UK and internationally, and many individuals and organisations internationally are working tirelessly to protect and restore these essential and beautiful meadows. Looking after our ocean is now acknowledged as a vital part of what is now known in policy circles as 'nature-based solutions' – using the recovery of nature to help to reduce climate change and adapt to its effects. Seagrass beds are beautiful, biodiverse habitats that directly sustain millions of livelihoods and protecting them brings us a wealth of benefits.

Some dives are more dramatic than others. In 2007 I was in the shallow, sheltered waters of Laxey Bay under the dramatic cliffs of Garwick. These dives were to survey for scallops after a reseeding exercise a few weeks earlier. Hundreds of baby scallops with numbered tags glued on were scattered from the fisheries protection vessel *Barrule* and we needed to check they'd settled on the seabed. We also had a good idea of the location of an inshore eelgrass meadow and were exploring the edges of that too. The inner bay was protected as a fisheries closed area (to allow scallop populations to recover from over-fishing) and additional ecological information would also help inform the future management of the area.

We had a rough plan, to do our fifty-metre transect, paying particular attention to scallops and habitat. Near the beginning of the dive my dive buddy started to pick up the odd bit of coal. Coal on the seabed is often the sign of an historic shipwreck – either the cargo of boats that didn't make it into port, or paddle steamers that sank with their fuel unburnt. I kept my eyes open for the dark pebbles worn smooth by over a century on the seabed and other evidence of shipwreck while I recorded the ecological information. I was scribbling in pencil on my white plastic slate – seabed type, habitat and any creatures on the bottom or in the water column. Sometime in the first half of the dive the current began to pick up. It was taking us offshore. Gradually we were forced to stop swimming against it and relaxed into moving with the tide.

Then, emerging from the sand ripples on the seabed I began to see arching black crescents. I managed to hang on to a rocky outcrop long enough to have a closer look and saw that it was clearly a bivalve, shell a little open like someone just about to speak, with reddish-gold flesh exposed and the distinctive pale siphon visible. I'd never seen one underwater before, but the thick black shells could only really be ocean quahog. Scientists now use the information encapsulated in the shells of these long-lived and elusive molluscs to recreate historic climates. They are the longest-lived non-colonial animals on earth and one Icelandic specimen was found to be 507 years old. I touched my buddy's arm with my black-gloved hand and pointed. He turned and swam into the current to inspect the shell and then raised his eyebrows at me inside his mask. Concentrating on spotting and recording the quahogs as we flew over them became the perfect distraction to my mounting concern about how far and how deep this current would take us.

Laxey Bay had seemed calm and sheltered as we'd gone into the water but the speed at which we were moving meant that I'd no idea where we might end up. As the current picked up, I glanced at my buddy every so often. He seemed completely at ease, pointing out the quahogs and still picking up the odd piece of coal, and popping it into his buoyancy control device (BCD) pockets.

I was breathing more quickly now. My air was beginning to get low. I showed my dive buddy my gauge. He signalled to me for another five minutes. I concentrated on breathing more slowly to conserve my air. Now, in places we were coming across little clusters of quahogs, three or four together. By now I felt like marine tumbleweed, tipping and twisting and trying to keep my gauges and my limbs in some sort of order.

Our ascent wasn't easy. I was conscious we were difficult for the boat to spot. I'm always afraid of being hit by propellors, so I was trying to make a controlled ascent in the current, while constantly keeping an eye up above. I was breathing rapidly and tense with concentration. At the surface we were looking back at the bay, well outside its sheltered confines and out in open water. But the boat spotted us quickly and we were soon on board. When we looked on the map later, we'd travelled over two kilometres in forty minutes. And we'd discovered a thriving and very rarely seen population of the most long-lived creatures on the planet. These dark molluscs may have been filtering plankton in Laxey Bay when Shakespeare's plays were first being performed and the population of Laxey spoke only Manx Gaelic and wouldn't have understood a word of them. Steaming back to Port St Mary we drank sweet tea and talked quahogs and drift dives all the way home.

5

Marine Conservation

'Our Island is small in area, but there are a lot of tucks in it: so many that a person could spend years exploring them and still have surprises in store.'

Mona Douglas, *This Is Ellan Vannin Again: Folklore*, 1966

It is November 2008 and I'm in a big meeting room at the Villa Marina, the Island's largest entertainment venue on Douglas promenade. It's a basement room so we can't see the dishcloth-grey waters of Douglas Bay just across the road, but the sea is the topic of conversation. We're here to launch the three-year project to create the very first Marine Nature Reserve on the Isle of Man. The walls of the room are covered in sheets of flipchart paper with maps of the Isle of Man decorated with exuberant circles, arrows and exclamations, and elsewhere lists and diagrams that provide more sober summaries of group discussions. Over a hundred people are dispersed across the rooms in groups and each group has two facilitators – one leading the discussion and the other recording the points that people are making. As I listen in to snatches of conversation in each group, I can hear bridges being built. A professor listens to a fisherman talking about the seasonality of queenie fishing. A harbour manager talks to an environmentalist about basking sharks. A diver enthuses about the sea to an office-bound civil servant. The workshop has been designed to do exactly this — to give everyone a chance to participate and to be heard, and to build a common purpose. In the foyer of the Villa Marina is a set of display boards with the participants' vision for 2020, scribbled on yellow sticky notes as they have arrived. Many of the notes evoke a sea that is leaping with life and vitality; puffins, sand eels and dolphins abound. They imagine a future network of Marine Nature Reserves that protect marine life and allow people to make a living from the sea. There are a lot of images of wind turbines and marine renewable energy, and acknowledgements of the increasing relevance of climate change in that future that seemed so far away at the time. Marine litter was also highlighted as a concern and the future imagined had beaches that were litter-free and safe from pollution. A common theme around that collective vision for the future was around the presence of people on the coast, on the sea and beneath the waves — kayakers, climbers, fishermen. One note envisions 'a Marine Nature Reserve that is used by all and provides a ring of protection around the Island'; another imagines 'standing on the shore with my 14-year-old son, flatfish scurrying for cover under his feet'. The majority of the comments are around building a positive future — 'healthy and protected', 'a sea with a future I am proud of'. But there is also fear of climate change and its impacts, with one comment hoping for a 'temperate climate. No further rise in sea level/temperature.'

I had started my job as the Isle of Man Government's first marine conservation officer in September 2004, a year after I'd arrived back. The job may have been brand new, but our place of work was steeped in the Island's history. Our office was based in part of a bull shed at Knockaloe Farm on the west coast of the Island. The farm had been the site of the Knockaloe Camp where over 23,000 German, Austrian and Turkish men were interned during the First World War. They were all people who had been living in Britain when war was declared with Germany and who became 'enemy aliens'. The most famous resident of the camp was perhaps Joseph Pilates who developed his pro-gramme of body-strengthening exercises there while he was interned between 1915 and 1919. When I worked there all that marked out the remarkable (and in many ways traumatic) past of Knockaloe was a plaque on a wall of one of the farm buildings and, in the small churchyard in Patrick village, some graves of internees who died during their incarceration. There is now a visitor centre across the road and many more people are aware of what happened there and its historical significance.

Knockaloe Farm near Peel. My office was the one nearest the camera (the bull shed was on the other side).

Popular British/Manx author Hall Caine wrote a novel, published in 1923, called *The Woman of Knockaloe* about the daughter of the farmer at Knockaloe who falls in love with a German internee in the camp and is disgraced. The story ends tragically but the book includes some lovely descriptions of Knockaloe and the surrounding area:

> Too far inland to hear the roar of the sea except in winter, it is near enough to feel its salt breath in the summer. Not rich or leafy or luxuriant, but with a broad sunny bareness as of a place where a glacier has been and passed over, and with a deep peace, a glacial peace, always lying on it – such is Knockaloe.

To get to the office you had to walk through a farmyard and you could often hear the bulls next door. The office was surrounded by rolling hills near the coast just south of Peel and hares often sprinted up and down the long drive as you drove to and from the office. Either side of the drive is an unusual stone wall which is made from the broken-up concrete floors of the huts where internees lived. On the way to the office is a tall, barn-like building which was actually one of the locomotive sheds from when a railway ran all the way to the internment camp. While most of the graves of German citizens were moved to a German military cemetery in England, some remain, with inscriptions in Hebrew and Turkish.

It was strange to work in a place like that, that had once been such an important part of history, a desperately sad place for the thousands of men interned there who had no idea when they would see their families again or when they would regain their freedom, but also where, through amazing determination and ingenuity, those men had made the best of the situation and kept healthy and active and productive. While not as famous as artists like Kurt Schwitters who was interned in Douglas during the Second World War, the internees held art exhibitions and many paintings and artefacts still remain. A kind of scrimshaw carved in cow bone was popular and some of these are on display in the Leece Museum in nearby Peel. There was a theatre, and plenty of professional actors and musicians to perform. One orchestra of at least forty members was also reported. Courses were available up to university level and a camp newspaper ran for a short time.

Many of the men had left Germany as small children and spoke no German and felt they had little connection with the land of their birth. All the same, they were separated from their families (women were not interned) and many weren't released from the camp until late in 1919, when reportedly many were deported to Germany, a country they had all left a long time before and of which many had no memory.

This sad piece of Manx history has been well documented elsewhere, but still seems too little known, both in the Isle of Man and more widely. One can only imagine the thousands of personal tragedies that went on for those people. The decision to detain those men of German and other 'enemy' heritage seems to have been directly related to the torpedoing of the British ship *Lusitania* too. Violence against German nationals erupted in communities across the UK and led to an order for all men of military age to be interned and all those who were older than that to be returned to Germany. The original capacity of Knockaloe was increased from 5000 to 10,000 and subsequently reached over 23,000.

Despite its troubled history, Knockaloe was a lovely place to work. I had the perfect commute – a drive along empty roads up over the southern uplands of the Island and along the west coast. When I drove in early to go for a swim in nearby Peel before work, I had to be careful of birds in the road, and I often felt as though I was the first person to have driven that way in the morning.

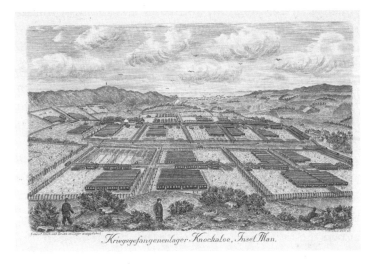

Kriegsgefangenenlager·Knockaloe, Insel Man.

A postcard of Knockaloe Camp from the collection of the
Knockaloe Charitable Trust.

The farm was the site for the Manx Wildlife Trust's native
wildflower nursery so there was always a bloom of colour
on my way in. We shared the farm location with the
government agriculture officers and it was a lovely rural
setting. In those early years I learnt a lot about conservation
on land, something I'd studied as part of my degree but not
been involved in since. My colleagues were working on
the selection of Areas of Special Scientific Interest, working
with farmers on management agreements to maximise the
biodiversity value of their land and enforcing the Wildlife
Act which protects wild birds and other species.

Near Knockaloe I was spoilt for magical places to walk
or swim before or after work, and occasionally on my
rare lunch breaks. After years away from the Island I really

appreciated the proximity to the sea and the opportunity to explore the Manx coastline again. Less conscious of my carbon footprint than I am now, I would sometimes drive ten minutes into Peel and park at Fenella beach. This little beach has formed over the centuries on one side of the causeway connecting Peel harbour with St Patrick's Isle, where the red sandstone walls of Peel Castle tower above the outer harbour. Decades of the dumping of scallop shells from the seafood-processing factories over the nearby cliffs of Peel Hill have resulted in a mosaicked beach almost completely made up of a jumble of white, pink and orange fragments of shell in place of pebbles. When the tide is high the white shell shingle beneath the surface gives the beach a tropical turquoise hue, making it a popular spot for photographers. I would sometimes crunch across the jigsaw pieces of scallop shell, up some steps hewn into the rocks at the side of the beach, and around the weather-worn walls of the castle that in the eleventh century was the fort of the Viking King of Mann Magnus Barelegs. An archaeological dig that was going on when I was growing up really captured my imagination. In 1984 the work revealed one of the most celebrated Viking burial sites in the British Isles, the grave of a wealthy Viking woman accompanied by many fascinating belongings, buried around AD 950. She became known as the Pagan Lady. There was speculation that she may have been some sort of sorceress and it was her necklace that made the biggest impression on me. The seventy-three beads came from all parts of the Viking kingdoms of her time – amber, jet and multi-coloured glass – linking her to the Baltic, southern Europe and the Middle East. As I looked out from the walls and over the clumps of sea pink and the tide flowing out down the tiered rockpools, I liked to imagine the sea journeys this woman had taken to and from Peel, over 1000 years before.

While I was really focused on the need to get the Marine Nature Reserve work under way, I wanted to learn from the negative Calf of Man response and put plenty of groundwork in to inform and involve as many people as possible in the process. I initiated a broad campaign of marine education and awareness raising which allowed me to get to know many of the key players in Manx marine life, from fishermen to conservationists. Lectures in church halls and articles in the local paper led to being put in contact with so many interesting people with connections to the sea and a wealth of local knowledge. I could then build on this to begin the development of the Marine Nature Reserves.

Setting up Marine Nature Reserves was by no means the only objective of my job. As the marine conservation officer, I had to pick up everything to do with looking after the sea. This ranged from considering potential marine developments and what their environmental impact might be, to recording and assessing dead seals and other marine mammals washed up around the Island to determine their cause of death. In the early years as I worked with my boss Liz and other colleagues to develop the marine conservation programme, I was lucky enough to work on so many topics. I was happy to work long hours and be on call for all sorts of interesting marine wildlife emergencies. If a dead seal, harbour porpoise or more rarely a whale or a dolphin was washed up dead on the shore, the police control room or the coastguard would give me a call and I'd go and check it out. Outside office hours I didn't have access to a work vehicle so I would turn up in my own car. I did have a work waterproof with the government logo on it, but I didn't always have it with me. On one occasion I was called out to inspect a dead porpoise while I was out and about doing something else at the weekend. It was winter and I turned up in a much-loved shin-length beige Norwegian sheepskin coat that my friend Julie had got from a charity shop in York and then passed on to me (to my delight) because she decided the sleeves were a bit too short for her. When I got to the carcass of the poor harbour porpoise washed up on the beach at Langness, I started taking photos and measuring the carcass to get the basic details that we passed on to a UK marine mammal stranding project. The carcass, as is often the case, was starting to decompose and had been pecked by gulls. It was difficult to determine whether it had been injured before death. A key observation with stranded harbour porpoises is the thickness of their blubber. Starvation through lack of their preferred sand eel prey, which is rich in oils and more highly calorific than other fish they eat, is relatively common now. As I started to take the measurements, I was chatting to a man at the scene who had also been taking photographs. I obviously didn't introduce myself properly because after a bit he said tentatively, 'Don't you think we should call the authorities?' He was quite surprised when I told him that I, in my ancient car and my sheepskin coat, was the authorities, and I don't think that he was convinced that I wasn't just someone with a strange penchant for dead marine mammals. After that I always tried to remember to bring my birdwatcher-green work anorak with me in the car. (When I had to find a new car in 2009 my main priority was to make sure that a dead porpoise would fit in the back, which gives you an insight into the focus of my life in my mid-thirties.)

Outreach was also a big part of my job. I always remember my first visit to a primary school where I'd been invited in to talk about sea life. Port St Mary is a fishing village with a strong maritime tradition. It is perched on the southern tip of the Isle of Man, just the other side from Port Erin, and the two villages remind me of a gateway to the wider southern Irish Sea. Their small harbours have seen the start of many important journeys, whether that has been trips just half an hour or so south of the Calf of Man, or much longer journeys by yachts or fishing boats or research vessels. Many of the houses in Port St Mary are near the sea or in sight of the sea and the whole village does have a maritime feel. So I should have been more prepared for the class of mini marine biologists who let me speak for a while and then bombarded me with their amazing sea experiences. Many of them talked about going fishing with parents or others off the flat limestone rocks that jut out from Port St Mary on one side. Those fishing experiences had given them close encounters with mackerel and pollack and conger eels, very like my own first experiences of marine life in close-up out fishing with my dad. Others had spent long summers on the beach rockpooling and beachcombing and talked about the lobsters their dads had found (rockpooling dads, I have learnt, are extremely competitive about things like lobsters – the charismatic megafauna of the tidepool). These children had seen Risso's dolphins and sunfish, and they'd heard stories about people seeing leatherback turtles. They were steeped in sea life and didn't really need my PowerPoint slides about basking sharks and turtles the size of cars. They were living it.

In the first few years working for the Isle of Man Government I had to make the difficult transition from idealistic researcher influencing on a global level to a small-island civil servant struggling to understand why the necessary bureaucracy of government can mean that everything can seem to happen in slow motion. This was a real learning experience and reinforced for me how marine ecology is only one small part of marine conservation. Ecology is complex and unpredictable and people even more so.

I spent a lot of time planning the Manx Marine Nature Reserve project. After all the initial reservations which had been raised, even from marine conservationists, I was very cautious about how to proceed. When it came to getting the approval to go ahead, I had planned out the consultation and research required to really get the community involved, and hopefully onside.

After the Calf of Man setback when the Marine Nature Reserve proposal had been subject to intense debate, getting the fishermen on board was a top priority, so we met with them before meeting any other stakeholders. We gave them the background for the project, the environmental need to protect our valuable habitats and the intention to ensure that the Marine Nature Reserves would bring benefits to their fisheries, through providing safe havens for king scallops to grow to larger sizes and produce plenty of young that could settle on their fishing grounds. We talked about the wider benefits of healthy ecosystems. In turn, the fishermen explained to us the complex set of pressures they were under. They outlined the proliferation of marine developments in the Irish Sea; their increasing costs and the low prices paid for seafood; the regulation and bureaucracy. All of these things were putting the industry under increasing pressure. It was challenging enough for them already without worrying about how our project could reduce the fishing grounds available to them, and impact on their options. I understood these concerns and it was my job to make the reserves work for fishermen as well as for nature.

In these discussions, as elsewhere, the fishing industry was passionate and vocal. There has been a lot of discussion in the UK and globally about whether the loud voice that the fishing industry has is proportionate to the size of the industry. Growing up by the sea, in a historically fishing-dependent community, I see that rather differently. Fishing has a key role in our coastal heritage, our culture and our stories of what it means to live by and off the sea. And of all those who use the sea, it is fishermen who are most impacted by marine management decisions. From that perspective, it is right that fishing is seen as a key issue and that fishermen have a voice. But I also think that advocacy for marine conservation and marine ecosystems needs to be stronger and the voices for the ocean heard, especially those that go beyond the dolphins and whales and advocate for the less glamorous species and habitats.

In my view this is beginning to balance out now. One really important reason for that is the growing understanding that healthy marine ecosystems have the potential to make an enormous difference in our efforts to tackle climate change. In the Isle of Man, balancing protection and use of the environment is all caught up in the fragility of small-island economies and our not-so-distant memories of harder times in the 1970s and '80s. Around the world there has long been a perception that you can either have a vibrant economy or look after your environment and lose all sorts of economic opportunities. The new way of thinking that is gradually filtering through is putting a healthy environment at the heart of a healthy economy, but this approach is still not widespread, and around the world decisions are still being made solely on the economic case.

When I did my training as a biologist and ecologist the emphasis was very much on the scientific skill set, but as a marine conservationist it is the human side that has been infinitely more important. The training for ecologists and conservationists now is much more focused on the people side of things. There is a big push to put marine social science on a par with the biology to inform better marine management. One of the most important skills I've learnt to help with marine conservation is empathy. It isn't until you've really thought long and hard about how it feels to be a fisherman who believes his livelihood is being directly threatened by conservation that you can begin to build bridges and make a difference.

It was that disconnect between the ecology and people side of things that we aimed to address with the work we were doing in 2008, at the workshop in the Villa Marina.

While most people scribbled down their thoughts for a positive vision of the future, one participant who was disillusioned with the process came to our reception desk in the foyer and wrote CODSWALLOP in capitals on a sticky note and left again. Fishermen and other stakeholders had concerns, and over the years I spent a lot of time talking to them, in particular their representatives in the Manx Fish Producers' Organisation. It was natural that fishermen were wary. Unlike farming where farmers either own or rent the land they work, and therefore largely have control over their own activities, within the restrictions set down around animal welfare, planning restrictions and the conditions of their subsidies and other government support, fishermen are exploiting a common resource that belongs no more to them than it does to any of us. So, a fisherman can invest heavily in a fishing boat, the relevant quotas (which can be very expensive) and licences but his operations could be stopped at any time by new legislation or by other uses of the sea. This is one reason why fishermen need strong unions and co-operatives to represent them. For centuries, fishing, alongside shipping, has been one of the main uses of the sea, but in the past two decades it has become a very busy place.

Since the North Hoyle Offshore Wind Farm came into operation in Liverpool Bay in 2003, there has been a rapid proliferation of ever taller, elegant, white-bladed wind farms popping up around the Irish Sea, providing the renewable energy that is essential for our low-carbon future. Other uses of the sea have intensified. In some areas sand and gravel are removed from the seabed for industrial uses. Gas platforms dominate the skyline as the Manx ferry approaches Heysham port, marking the sites where large volumes of methane gas are extracted from under the Irish Sea, where it has been trapped for hundreds of millions of years. With the expansion of offshore wind and the need for more interconnection between electricity grids and for telecommunications, the Irish Sea is increasingly criss-crossed with cables and interconnectors too.

It is no wonder that most fishermen initially saw Marine Nature Reserves as just another problem, another claim on their territory and a competing use of the sea.

Even so, other than the 'codswallop' incident there was a supportive and positive feel to the workshop, and it felt like real progress. The sticky notes and maps from that meeting went on to inform an Island-wide consultation. We made the decision to go to every community in the Island and so my colleague Laura and I spent a few weeks in January and February 2009 running public meetings in every town and village. We became experts in setting up display boards in record time and navigating the kitchens of church halls and community centres (always bring your own tea towels). Instead of expecting people to travel to Douglas for meetings we went to them, and I'm sure lots of people who wouldn't otherwise have got involved came along to a meeting in their village or town. While the format for our consultation meetings was the same at each event, the atmosphere and outcomes of the evenings could not have been more varied.

In Port St Mary we had a busy meeting in the large Methodist church hall. I recognised a lot of the people who had packed into the hall which is just round the corner from the harbour – there were fishermen, anglers, divers, marine biologists and boat operators. In the community closest and most connected to the Calf of Man, the old animosities from the failed Calf of Man Marine Nature Reserve proposal (sixteen years earlier) rose to the surface and I had the feeling that some of the players from that debate were back in character and ready for a replay. At that meeting my personal involvement in the project was highlighted and one older man who was opposed to Marine Nature Reserves had found a marine reserve management plan I'd written with colleagues in the Indian Ocean island of Rodrigues and starting reading extracts and asking if I was going to do something similar in the Isle of Man.

Things were a little less heated in Port Erin where the tiered seats of the Erin Arts Centre were filled, again with a mixture of those with a general interest and those with close links to the sea. The personal connection made at this meeting came from another older man who remembered my fisherman great-grandfather and said that our proposals would help protect seals around the Calf of Man, and that my great-grandfather would have shot the seals to stop them competing with his fishing. I've no idea if this was true (I've asked around and it seems very unlikely), but I do know that in my great-grandfather's time, seal numbers around the Calf were reportedly much lower than they are now and also that my dad's family fished mainly for crab and lobster, so the conflict with seals would have been less of an issue. At the time I was living in Port Erin and this meeting felt incredibly personal to me. I knew many of the people who'd come to the event and was living four minutes' walk up the promenade and I was being challenged in public about my ancestors killing wildlife. However, I knew that the alternative, if I was not a Manx scientist with a fishing heritage, would have been accusations of coming in as a stranger and telling the locals what to do, so on the whole I took these personal digs in good humour. I was still determined to keep reaching out and engaging people, especially those who felt the most threatened by what we were trying to do.

In Laxey in a small community room run by the local football club, an old friend of my dad's who he played football with at Liverpool University introduced me at the meeting. There weren't many people at that event but those who were there were interested and enthusiastic. There was an environmental science student back visiting his family, the parents of an old marine biologist friend and lots of other people with links to the sea or a general interest in its future. At Peel, a town a bit like Ramsey where there is still a strong sense of community and where fishing still feels like a big influence, we were really pleased to see lots of younger people. My colleague Laura was living in Peel at the time and she had encouraged her friends to come along. Loyal followers of our previous marine events were also there.

The most positive meeting by far was the one we held in Ramsey, the second-biggest town in the Isle of Man and separated to some extent from the rest of the Island by a range of hills. It was held in the upstairs meeting room at the town hall, somewhere I've held and attended many meetings over the years. The room was packed and the atmosphere was positive. The main theme that people kept returning to was their concern that because Ramsey sewage was still pumped untreated into the bay, that there could never be a Marine Nature Reserve there. By now it was 2009 and I'd not lived in Ramsey since I'd left eighteen years earlier to go to university, but my parents still lived there and I was a regular visitor. When I was there for evening events I'd usually stay at my parents' house. (This is a very Isle of Man response to travelling for an hour which is about the maximum you can do on an Island thirty miles long – I could obviously have driven home the same evening but something definitely happens to your sense of distance when you live on a small island.) At the time we knew that the sewage issue was going to be dealt with soon (a big sewage treatment infrastructure project was under way). We left the meeting feeling very positive about what could be achieved and I felt secretly very proud that it was my own home town that was embracing this project most enthusiastically. Over the years it had become so important to me, and it felt like a good sign that it might finally become reality.

Alongside the public consultation where we learnt about the importance of places to the people who used and enjoyed them, and anecdotal information about where fish spawned or reefs frequented by octopus, we were also gathering together recent and more historic scientific information about the Manx marine environment. During this time I learnt so much more about the sea I had grown up beside and it transformed in my imagination as I walked the coastal paths and began to develop a much clearer view, in my mind's eye at least, of the shape of the seabed and animals and plants that occupied it.

At weekends I would walk from my cottage down Port Erin promenade to go shopping in the local supermarket and I could pause on the brooghs overlooking the bay to watch gannets diving sleek and purposeful, feeding on sand eels and other small fish. Now I could imagine the sandy furrows across the bay, with juvenile plaice scudding between them and the thriving seabed of the Port Erin closed area, rich in delicate branching hydroids and super-sized king scallops. I could picture the writhing tangle of a brittlestar bed, alive with robotic yet graceful legs reaching for fragments of detritus floating past, and the occasional golden flourish of a rare flame shell, its orange fringe of tentacles like an anemone trapped inside a shell.

On my lunchtime walks in Peel I could look out for the puffins flying out to sea from Contrary Head, and go at low tide to see the blue mussel beds on the shore at Fenella beach and look under ledges to find the clustered yellow dog whelk eggs. From the harbourside I could watch for the black guillemot nesting in the holes in the old harbour wall, immediately identifiable by their bright red feet.

I could escape from a meeting in government offices and be up on Marine Drive in a few minutes, looking north to the busy port of Douglas with the ferry returning from Heysham and fishing boats steaming back after a day at sea, with maerl beds and kelp forests just tens of metres from the curved promenade of Victorian hotels. To the south I could look down over the cliffs to where the biodiverse wealth of Little Ness horse mussel reef lay hidden, with the hope of seeing the blunt head of a Risso's dolphin emerging or a fleeting glimpse of a harbour porpoise surfacing.

Venturing further afield on a weekend walk down a narrow path through the bracken to the ruins of a *keeill* and tiny hermit's cell at Lag ny Keeilley on the south-west coast, I could picture the maerl beds offshore providing food-rich nurseries for young cod and waving forests of kelp. From that dramatic vantage point on the slopes of Cronk ny Arrey Laa, far from any settlements and high above the sea, I might glimpse a basking shark fin disappearing in the wide glimmering of ocean stretching out to Ireland, invisible in the haze.

From the jaunty red and white stripes of the Point of Ayre lighthouse in the north to the dour grey of the Chicken Rock lighthouse a few miles south-west of the Calf of Man, the seas around the Island were revealing their mysteries to me through science, survey and the stories of the people who knew them best. What I was learning far exceeded my expectations. We had so much to celebrate and so much to protect.

6

Ocean Giants

'. . . I count as gain
That once I met, on a sea tin-tacked with rain,
That room-sized monster with a matchbox
brain.'

Norman MacCaig, 'Basking Shark', 1967

It's July 2008. We're three miles off Peel and just about to head back to Port St Mary when I see the fin approaching. We've been at sea all day; red-faced with sun and wind, and weary. We've tagged three female basking sharks. We could identify each one by nicks on the dorsal fin or on the tail. We've photographed them and Graham has attached the red satellite tags at the base of the fin with a deft spearing technique he has perfected over years. Two sharks barely noticed but the third twitched sharply as if stung, giving us a quick sweep of the tail before diving.

The sea has been flat the whole day long and barely laps the boat as we drift. Graham has been getting the boat ready for us to set off for home, I've put my notebook away and Duncan is packing up his camera. But this fin is big and we all stop what we are doing to watch. A dorsal fin, over a metre tall, so large it flaps over on itself like a puppy's ear. It's impossible to predict what a shark will do. Some are curious and will approach and others make a rapid exit when they detect a boat. And there's always the possibility that it will breach, heaving its vast bulk completely clear of the surface before crashing down again. In the Clyde in the 1930s a whole family was lost at sea when a breaching shark capsized their boat.

This shark continues to swim in our direction. Swiftly and purposefully, in graceful zigzag lines, the vast fish gets nearer. Through the clear water I can see the white gape of the mouth and the darker gill slits. And all at once, it's under us. Instinctively I jump back, away from the side of the boat. Underneath us is a creature bigger than a bus, at least nine metres long, among the biggest ever seen in our waters. We regularly see sharks of five or six metres, but this is unusual. Just below the water, I can see its sun-dappled grey skin so clearly, rough like coarse sandpaper. Its back is broad, much wider than the boat. It's of a different scale to any other creature that I've seen before, and more ancient. In the boat, we seem so small and flimsy.

It cruises beneath. The only sound comes as the tail fin breaks the surface on the other side of the boat and sea drips from the fin leaving a trail of circles perfectly formed. It seems unreal.

That shark is etched on my brain. Though I've kept close company with other large beasts, none compares. A humpback whale in the Pacific Ocean, just visible in the murk and singing. Elephants munching wheelbarrow mouthfuls of grass in Tanzania, always a safe distance away in that ancient savannah landscape, with vultures circling overhead. Like the immediate connection I felt to the acacia-dotted wilds of Lake Manyara, the impact of that unexpected encounter accessed something prehistoric. Sharks first evolved around 450 million years ago and the basking shark emerged much later, in the Eocene era, between 56 and 33 million years ago. Early sharks shared the planet with dinosaurs and could have been hunted by the ichthyosaurs whose remains are now on display in the Natural History Museum in London, discovered by the fossil hunter Mary Anning. Gradually those marine predators have vanished into evolutionary time and now the only species to really pose a threat to basking sharks is us.

The giant shark we saw was a male, its long claspers visible beneath the body. The equivalent of a pair of metre-long penises, the claspers inseminate the female who after up to three years' gestation will give birth to two or more live young. Basking sharks don't mature until they are at least six years old and then produce their young so slowly. This approach to reproduction means that it's no surprise they're struggling globally – they are often accidentally caught before they've had a chance to reproduce once. While many countries now protect basking sharks, they are still captured deliberately for their fins on the high seas and areas outside national jurisdictions. In the Atlantic, they are currently protected outside national waters by an international agreement, but they remain under threat. In 2019 they were recategorised by the International Union for Conservation of Nature (IUCN) as endangered. This assessment means they are at very real risk of extinction in the near future.

A basking shark feeding at the surface.

In the Isle of Man, people get very excited about basking sharks. There are few mentions of basking sharks in Manx history and folklore and it's very difficult to know whether they only really appeared in great numbers in the 1960s when records of their presence in Manx waters begin to appear, or whether it was just a case of them being such a common part of the seascape that no one felt the need to record them. In 1840 a lecture by Edward Forbes was reported in the *Manx Sun* where he talked about basking sharks being not uncommon off the west coast of Ireland but no mention was made of their prevalence around the Isle of Man. A report on the Manx involvement in the Kinsale mackerel fishery in another local newspaper, the *Mona's Herald*, in 1871 mentioned Manx fishermen's nets being damaged by a basking shark that had been accidentally caught. My grandmother lived her whole life looking over Port Erin Bay, now an acknowledged basking shark hotspot, but she only remembered one occasion when she saw a basking shark close up, on a picnic boat trip round Bradda Head to Fleshwick Bay when she was a child in the 1920s.

In 2009 we had a bumper year for basking sharks in the Isle of Man. Licensing the tagging and filming of basking sharks was part of my job as marine conservation officer, which was a great excuse to get out to sea once in a while. Since 2004 Manx Basking Shark Watch has coordinated a citizen science project, encouraging the public to report any basking shark sightings online. Whether they are seen from cliffs on a coastal walk or encountered close up in a kayak, all sightings provide useful data that can help scientists understand the wanderings of this beast. Over 500 sightings of sharks were reported in 2009, the highest count by a long way. Sightings ranged from groups of up to thirty adults, feeding offshore on plankton aggregating in the coastal fronts, to individual juveniles (even they are over two metres long) languishing in shallow coves an arm's reach from the rocks. What were assumed to be courting pairs of full-sized adults danced circles around one another. They curled and zigzagged and seemed to chase their own and each other's tails. In recent years, there've not been so many and nobody is sure if this is a real decline in numbers or just natural variation as migration patterns change from year to year. A ground-breaking genetics paper published in 2020 by shark geneticists Dr Lilian Lieber, Prof. Les Noble, Dr Catherine Jones and their team, and using data collected by Jackie and Graham Hall of Manx Basking

Shark Watch, estimated total numbers of basking sharks in the whole of the North-East Atlantic to be less than 10,000 and between 241 and 830 basking sharks using the Irish Sea on a regular basis.

Basking sharks have tiny brains (variously described as the size of a tangerine, a Mars bar or by Norman MacCaig, in what is perhaps my all-time favourite poem, as a match-box) but very sensitive noses which they use to detect their prey. What they are searching for is rich patches of small shrimps called *Calanus*, a type of plankton. These shrimps are sensitive to temperature, with two main species present. In the waters of the British Isles, the cooler-water one – *Calanus finmarchicus* – has declined, while the warmer-water species – *Calanus helgolandicus* – has increased. Nobody really knows how changes in prey availability and distribution and other results of climate change will impact on basking sharks. They have a wide geographic distribution but are generally thought of as a cooler-water species, so their range could be compressed by rising sea temperatures and there will inevitably be impacts on their behaviour.

Basking sharks are a common visitor to the Isle of Man and other hotspots in the British Isles, including Cornwall, the west of Scotland and around the north of Ireland. For decades they have been a mystery to scientists, but now new technology such as satellite tagging, which can relay in almost real time the global travels of animals, is revealing much about these beasts. Satellite tags have shown that basking sharks dive to depths of over 10,000 feet, they travel across oceans and they can also return to the same places to feed year after year. The tagging data has been magically enhanced by genetic studies. Slime collected painlessly from the rough skins of basking sharks contains enough genetic material for scientists to extract and fingerprint each animal. So, a shark tagged in the Isle of Man can have its DNA profiled and then a fuller picture emerges of what individuals and groups are doing. Sharks are renowned for being solitary creatures and like many fish aren't known for their parenting skills or family values. For a long time, scientists believed that though basking sharks do the mammal-like thing of giving birth, mother and pup probably just swam off in different directions. The genetic work tells a different story and in the Irish Sea, family groups of basking sharks are regularly recorded. This information has completely changed my perception of these matchbox-brained monsters. Not cold-blooded, oblivious, eating machines but cosy groups of relatives cruising after plankton in packs.

Two dorsal fins and a tail – two basking sharks swimming closely together.

Perhaps it was partly the perception of basking sharks as monsters that influenced the darkest period in their recent history. In the late nineteenth and early twentieth centuries basking sharks were widely hunted for their valuable liver oil. Hunting at a scale unimaginable today took place around hotspots like Achill Island off the west coast of Ireland and off the west of Scotland. Scientists hope that they are bouncing back from the brink of extinction but we still don't really know. They are also notoriously variable from year to year so it is very difficult to have confidence in trends.

A basking shark fin with a satellite tag just visible at the surface. Fins can be over a metre tall.

The tagging work is also revealing a lot about the migration of basking sharks around the British Isles. A shark named Tracy that was tagged in Manx waters in 2007 showed the shark dived deeper than previously recorded and remarkably, she crossed the Atlantic, almost reaching Canadian shores before the tag popped off. However, other tagged sharks have not been as adventurous and the majority of sharks seen in the Irish Sea probably don't move much further than the British Isles, remaining on the continental shelf and not straying into deep waters.

Despite our love of basking sharks in the Isle of Man, there are still conflicts. We love the sea, we love our basking sharks, but as a nation we also love motorsports (personally I avoid them whenever possible but it is almost taboo to admit this in the home of the TT races). In 2007 I was really concerned to hear, completely by chance, that planning was well underway to organise a high-speed powerboat race around the whole Island in mid-June, the height of the basking shark season. Manx Basking Shark Watch had just begun to collect data on basking sharks from public sightings and I knew the race would be going through some real hotspots where in some years basking sharks could gather in pairs for what we thought was courtship, or in much larger feeding groups. My point of contact on the local organising team was really helpful but seemed to be genuinely surprised that this could be a problem. His solution was for me to give a briefing to the powerboat drivers and the race organisers the day before the race was due to be held. I really wasn't happy with this solution but I was relatively new to government and there is always a desire to work together, so I agreed.

The day before, I phoned a marine conservation contact to talk it over, a basking shark expert from the Marine Conservation Society, who had visited the Isle of Man not long before and encouraged the Manx Wildlife Trust to promote their sightings scheme locally. He had worked on basking sharks for a long time and had done a lot to promote basking shark protection across the UK. He suggested making sure that the racing drivers were very clear about how big a basking shark was. Surely, he reasoned, if they realised the sheer size of the creatures, they would understand the risk to themselves. I prepared my presentation and included a clear slide showing the size of a basking shark, the size of a powerboat and the size of a bus.

I gave the briefing to a full lecture theatre at the Manx Museum: this is the basking shark season; they're bigger than a bus; you can't always see their fins, they can be just below the surface; if you crash into one it may be you that comes out worse. Also, they're legally protected and endangered internationally. I tried to sound matter of fact and practical. My audience listened with interest and agreed to a survey of the course before the race went ahead. Knowing that not seeing any fins during the survey would be no guarantee that no sharks were just below the surface, I hoped that they would see some fins. In the end I think someone got cold feet and the round-the-Island race was called off anyway in the morning and they confined their racing to Douglas Bay on the east of the Island which has seen very few basking sharks reported over the years. I was relieved on behalf of all those peacefully feeding basking sharks that weren't going to become part of a racecourse – and that the Isle of Man wasn't put on the map for the first known basking shark fatality in a motorsport event.

Adrenalin junkies have a lot to answer for. The thirst for

danger that drives people to run a really high risk of death by racing around the bumpy, tree-lined, spectator-filled roads of the Isle of Man may also have contributed to the global decimation of basking sharks. I had an insight into that thrill on the deck of that boat as that giant specimen cruised less than a metre away from me. I was buzzing for the rest of the day. I relived the moment over and over again. I told anyone who would listen.

In 2009, I worked with Jackie Hall from Manx Basking Shark Watch, Dr Mauvis Gore from Save our Seas and other colleagues to organise the world's first international basking shark conference. Delegates travelled from throughout the basking shark's global range and discussed the science and management of this creature. One of the most memorable stories told at the meeting was about the demise of basking sharks off the west coast of Canada. Salmon is big business in Canada and because the seasonal visits of basking sharks coincided with the salmon-fishing season, the sharks would tangle in the nets, destroying the fishing gear and the valuable catch. So, the Canadian government began a basking shark cull and fitted huge knives to the front of a fleet of ships which set out to kill basking sharks. The bloody history of basking sharks in British Columbia was documented in a book by Scott Wallace, who had continued to study the species in Canadian waters. He estimated that over a period of around fifty years between the 1920s and 1970s, thousands of sharks were intentionally killed. The carcasses were brought back to port and the livers extracted for oil.

On the other side of the Atlantic, at Achill Island off the west coast of Ireland, the purpose of the cull was the rich liver oil that was burnt to illuminate towns and villages. A basking shark's liver makes up over a third of its total body weight and represented a valuable resource for communities in Ireland. At Achill it is estimated that over 100,000 basking sharks were taken from the 1940s to the 1990s.

Author Gavin Maxwell, well known for his book *Ring of Bright Water*, also wrote vividly and disturbingly about hunting for basking sharks in Scotland in his earlier book *Harpoon at a Venture*. He had his initial experience of basking shark hunting in 1944 when he machine-gunned the first shark he'd ever seen. He spent the next five years hunting and killing sharks, as part of a commercial venture he established on the Hebridean island of Soay. For Maxwell it was the excitement of the chase, the thrill of hunting down an enormous ancient beast. While his descriptions of his time at sea are beautiful and haunting, his enthusiasm for butchering these animals is less appealing.

Basking shark hunting continued in Scotland until the 1980s. Howard McCrindle was the last Scottish basking shark hunter and has written about his experiences. I met Howard in the early 2000s when he had become the skipper for the research vessel at the Millport Marine Laboratory. I remember his account of the frosty reception he'd received in the Isle of Man when he brought his hunting vessel into Peel in the 1980s. Soon after I met him, he joined shark scientist Dr Mauvis Gore as the skipper for her Scottish basking shark research project and so his extensive knowledge of how to find a basking shark was used for good, to find and tag the sharks. Howard was not alone in searching for basking sharks in Manx waters.

In the 1970s Norwegian hunting vessels would sometimes land at Peel, big harpoons on the fronts of their vessels, like whaling ships. The Isle of Man didn't keep records of the numbers they took and it would be very useful to track this information down as it would provide a really useful context for today's basking shark science.

Manx fishermen, it seems, were never much into hunting basking shark. In the 1980s and '90s, while sharks were still being caught elsewhere, a basking shark recording programme led by local accountant Ken Watterson did a brilliant job in raising local awareness about basking sharks. Ken's research, assisted by many local volunteers over the years, provided enough information to ensure the Isle of Man was the first place in the British Isles to legally protect basking sharks, listing the species on the Wildlife Act in 1990. This work also provided evidence to support the protection of basking sharks under UK legislation in 1997.

Citizen science – members of the public collecting information that can be used to help scientists – has played an extraordinarily important role in research into basking sharks globally. The logistics of studying this elusive species are complex. While people have an idea of the seasons and conditions in which we can expect to see basking sharks, it is impossible to predict where and when they will turn up. The Manx Basking Shark Watch team have to be all set to get their boat out and get tagging as soon as reports start coming in of sharks in the water. For researchers who are not based where the basking sharks are, the logistics of deploying an expedition for tagging or other studies are so challenging because you never know when the sharks will turn up. But around the Isle of Man and at other basking shark hotspots, there are always plenty of people out on the water or around the coast who spot basking sharks and take photos of the fins that might be good enough to recognise an individual. New apps and websites allow observers to record not only the time and place but also crucially what the shark was doing.

People who regularly spend time on the coast can also help by reporting strandings of dead marine animals. Around the British Isles this is most often marine mammals like harbour porpoises and the occasional minke whale, but sometimes dead basking sharks strand on the shoreline. These sad discoveries can provide important insights into the biology of animals that it is rarely possible to study close up. For a long time it was part of my job to assess and record these dead strandings. So, in 2011 I had another memorable close encounter with a basking shark – a dead one. I got a call from someone on a boat who'd spotted something stranded on the west coast of the Island, close to a promontory of rocks called Niarbyl. The site was difficult to access. My colleague Laura and I got our strandings kit together, called our colleagues in Manx Basking Shark Watch and the local marine mammal group and set off to investigate. We had to get permission from the farmer who owned the land to walk across a few fields, then clamber down some low rocky cliffs, carefully avoiding angry nesting gulls, to an inlet where a basking shark carcass had come ashore. The shark had been floating at sea for a few days and the flesh was beginning to break away from the cartilaginous skeleton. Where the rough dark grey skin had broken, the flesh was pale pink, disturbingly similar to cooked salmon, and breaking into flakes in a similar way.

Returning to the stranded basking shark to get some more samples.

It sounds macabre, but I have always wanted the opportunity to examine a dead basking shark so part of me was elated. This was the first time I could get my hands on one of these animals I'd been working to conserve for years. It smelt as you'd expect a big dead fish to smell, but not as nauseating as the rotting whales and porpoises I dealt with more often. I felt the sandpaper skin I'd read about and seen from the surface, but never touched. I inspected the delicate gillrakers that sieve out the tiny shrimps from swimming pools of seawater they pump through their gills. Fine and white, the bunches of them were like hand-made fascinators. I could examine the tiny teeth, small as daisy petals. And the stomach contents poured out as we opened her up. Made up entirely of *Calanus*, the planktonic shrimp, they were red as tinned tomato soup and thick and oily as a rich curry.

Tiny basking shark teeth in a piece of jaw –
they are less than 1cm long.

Surveying the slumped form of the basking shark, left stranded uncomfortably over a protruding rock by the retreating tide, I also felt very sad. Why had this animal died? We couldn't tell from our rapid post-mortem and the bits and pieces we sent away for further tests didn't tell us any more. It was an adult, just over seven metres. Its stomach was full. It wasn't emaciated and there was no evidence that it had become tangled in ropes or hit by a boat – two possible causes of death for basking sharks in the British Isles.

Some good came from this loss. We removed the dorsal fin, took samples of the stomach contents, teeth and skin, and various bits were sent around the British Isles to the relevant experts. Because basking sharks are listed on the Convention on the International Trade in Endangered Species (CITES), every movement, even of a fragment of skin or a piece of jaw, must be permitted by the country it leaves and the country it arrives in. The dorsal fin was used by Graham to develop a new technique to attach the latest satellite tags to sharks.

This close encounter with a dead basking shark was a clear reminder to me of their vulnerability, despite their enormous size. The more we find out about them, the more astonishing it is that they have hung on and not succumbed to the relentless impact of humans. Now that people have been studying basking sharks around the Isle of Man for decades, patterns have begun to emerge. Basking sharks usually start to arrive when the sea reaches 12°C, which corresponds with the bloom of their shrimp plankton. But temperatures are changing. Since 1906 in Port Erin Bay in the Isle of Man, every morning at the same time someone would go down to the jetty in front of the Port Erin Marine Laboratory and take the temperature of the sea. It is automated now, but the data collection continues and we have over a hundred years of measurements. In just over a century, the seas have warmed by an average of over 1°C and this warming has accelerated rapidly in the last ten years. Of those last ten years, eight have been the hottest on record. Similar patterns are occurring worldwide, although sea temperatures vary greatly from place to place, and some regions are more affected by sea-temperature rise than others. All seas link into one global ocean and all things marine are interlinked. If temperatures are too high in spring, the plankton blooms but juvenile fish that feed on them may not have hatched. The cues are all askew and vital synchronicity is lost. Perfectly timed coincident events, honed through evolution, become mismatched. The plankton hatches but the predators are still in eggs or a stage behind in their migration.

What can we do? The interconnectedness is key. The consequences of making changes are unpredictable. Biologists Paul and Anne Ehrlich captured this in their rivet-popper hypothesis. When a plane is flying through the air you don't need to think about each nut and bolt, but each one plays a vital part and if you were to assemble the plane without just one of those components, the consequences could be disastrous. Working on the islands of the Seychelles, Prof. Nick Graham of Lancaster University has found that islands where rats have been eradicated, boosting bird populations and creating more natural habitats on land, also have healthier coral reefs. In St Lucia the demands of UK supermarkets that dictated how banana plantations were managed to reduce pests had a direct effect on the health of coral reefs and therefore on fisheries and the livelihoods of fishermen. So, we may not always know exactly what is required for healthy ecosystems but building diverse places bursting full of different species is known to build resilience. Rewilding, marine protected areas, habitat restoration – all these tools will help us build a world that is able to adapt to change. While active conservation of basking sharks may seem challenging, protecting them where they are breeding and giving birth and working towards healthier oceans can only do good. Recent research has also highlighted the importance of large marine animals like sharks and whales for storing carbon. The carcasses of these huge creatures, most of which end up at the bottom of the deep seas, represent a different form of blue carbon and play an important role in locking away carbon that would otherwise be released as carbon dioxide, exacerbating climate change.

If we are pessimistic, then along with coral reefs, basking sharks may be among the things that future generations never get to see. My son is now eight and he's seen basking sharks twice already even though his birth corresponded with the start of a period of low sightings of this iconic species around the Manx coast. The first time was when he was three on a boat trip around the Calf of Man Marine Nature Reserve at the southern extreme of the Isle of Man. The second time he was five and the shark was swimming just below the cliffs as we walked down to Port Erin village for a promised ice-cream. He was excited for a minute or so and then remembered the ice-cream and we moved on much sooner than I wanted. For him an enormous, slow-moving shark fin was nothing special. He's seen one before, we read about them a lot, he knows that they are endangered, like the Amazon river dolphins he'd just done a homework project on. But they are part of his landscape.

Basking sharks are often described in conservation circles as charismatic megafauna (big animals). Along with whales and dolphins, they are the beloved icons of our abundant ocean. We value these animals even if we've never seen them ourselves. In the basking sharks' bloody past we are reminded of what we are capable of as humans. And what we are doing now is no less brutal, just more insidious. Rising sea temperatures could squeeze animals like basking sharks into a narrow band in northern seas, and even then they may not be safe, their plankton prey arriving at the wrong time, their old migratory patterns lost.

In good years, basking sharks can be seen all around the south-west of the Isle of Man, but in my mind it is Peel, midway up the west coast of the Island, which is most closely associated with the sharks. It is where we've sometimes come in to refuel from days at sea tagging or filming basking sharks, sitting on plastic chairs in our oil-skins outside the little kiosk on the harbour eating greasy kipper baps. Over the years small boats have run basking shark tours from the harbour, so it has also seen the start of days when I've taken visitors out to see their first ever basking sharks, starting with the friendly seals that approach the boats as they leave the harbour and always framed in the dramatic layers of headlands and cliffs that extend south towards the Calf of Man, or the crumbling golden sand cliffs to the north. Peel's harbour is still full of fishing boats and the quaysides are strewn with nets and pots, but it is increasingly becoming a centre for recreation as well as working on the sea, a favourite launching spot for kayaks and pleasure boats.

On a warm summer's night in Peel the sun sets in an orange glow behind the sandstone ruins of Peel Castle, once a Viking stronghold and where in the 1980s archaeol-ogists found a vividly coloured necklace made from beads traded by Vikings across Europe and beyond. Around the bay, from the harbour wall to Fenella beach, people stand alone or in groups and everyone seems to be looking out to sea. Triangle fins, like children's drawings, dip and emerge from mercury waters and nobody on the shore can take their eyes off them. Some fins remain alone as the sharks cruise, sleek, across the bay. Others interact in pairs, and it is sometimes difficult to tell a fin from the tip of an enormous tail as they swirl and circle. From time to time, they dive and disappear completely, leaving the metallic skin of the sea intact. A kayaker appears from round the headland, with the slip and drip of paddles and then silence as they stop and let a shark approach. Silhouetted now beside the castle walls, human and shark pause together.

7

Ramsey Bay

'Ramsey Town, O Ramsey Town,
Shining by the sea,
Here's a health to my true love,
Wheresoe'er she be.'
Published in W.H. Gill's *Manx National Songs*, 1896

After years of preparation and then a full year of working
intensively with the community to create a conversation
about protecting our seas, we finally began to make progress
on the Marine Nature Reserve project. We worked with
people from all backgrounds in every town and village to
really understand people's concerns and the vision they had
for our seas. We spent a lot of time reviewing the wealth of
data on Manx marine life, insights into fishing activity and
studies of how different marine resources were currently
used. Working with scientists at Bangor University and
other research partners, we also collected and analysed new
data on the species and habitats around the coast from dive
surveys and boat surveys using drop-down cameras and
other technology. We looked back at Sue Gubbay's 2000

report and an earlier report by leading marine biologist Prof. Steve Hawkins that recommended sites for protection, and at MSc projects including a relatively recent one by Dr Maija Marsh who reviewed potential sites for protection. Eventually we came up with a long list of twenty-three sites that would benefit from protection and would meet international (OSPAR – the Oslo–Paris Convention for the Protection of the Marine Environment of the North-East Atlantic) criteria and put together a report on these to be considered by the Wildlife Committee, an advisory board on issues related to the Isle of Man Wildlife Act.

The next stage that we had planned was to do further work on these sites, with the communities that knew them best, and from a scientific perspective too to fill gaps in knowledge. We then planned to prioritise them based on the more detailed assessments and decide which site should be designated first. That was the plan anyway.

As the summer went on, though, in various conversations with fishing industry representatives Ramsey Bay began to be mentioned. The bay had been closed earlier in the year after heavy fishing pressure, and what was thought to have been damage to the nursery beds that sustained young scallops in the bay, which had led to a crash in king scallop populations. There were conversations about when this emergency closure might end and what was best in the long-term of the fishery, and somewhere along the way came the suggestion that maybe Ramsey could be the first Marine Nature Reserve that could benefit nature, have minimal short-term impact on fishing (because at least part of the ecologically important area was already closed) and also the potential for long-term fishery benefits.

Ramsey town and Bay from Albert Tower.

Well, yes it could. Ramsey Bay itself was one of our twenty-three priority sites and the horse mussel bed to the north in the Ballacash Channel was also on the list. We talked some more about this and after further discussions with stakeholders we started to think about it more seriously. Various meetings followed and a plan evolved. The emergency closure was due to end in November 2009. Ramsey Bay had a particularly rich mix of key habitats, with maerl beds, horse mussel reefs, kelp forests and eelgrass beds, and there was potential for these to be protected with the support of the fishing industry. One way to look at it was that by supporting Ramsey, an area that was already closed, the fishermen were avoiding giving up any further fishing grounds. This was true, but Ramsey was a rich fishing ground, and the emergency closure was always intended to be temporary. The other way to look at it was that this was a great opportunity to protect somewhere special that was teeming with wonderful diversity, with the support of the fishing industry and enormous potential to support the sustainability of the fisheries.

This is where working in a small place, with a small government, really comes into its own. The three-year plan for the Marine Nature Reserve project had been approved through various different processes and a range of commitments had been made. We'd started the intentionally slow, sensitive round of stakeholder engagement as part of a longer process. The next steps were mapped out. In a bigger place it may have been more difficult to change course, but once we had decided that this was the best way forward, we were able to revise our plans relatively quickly.

It did take quite a few months to get agreement, but eventually we'd got the necessary approvals to put the plan on hold and pursue the Ramsey Bay option with the fishing industry. We had numerous meetings with the fishermen to discuss the details. Together we pored over habitat maps showing the location of the maerl beds, the horse mussel reefs and the eelgrass alongside print-outs of fishing patterns built up from years of data from the fishing vessels. There were long discussions about finding the balance between keeping viable fishing grounds while at the same time protecting the most important areas of habitat. There had to be give and take on both sides and there were long negotiations about the places most valued for biodiversity and for fishing yields. It was some of the inshore maerl habitat that was thought to be of particular value to juvenile scallops. Protecting it all could make a big difference to the fishery, but it also reduced the grounds available to fish. Some of the more traditional Ramsey fishermen who had been fishing the bay for generations called an area to the north end of the bay the Garden, and that is where they believed the young scallops settled as they moved out of the plankton and onto the seabed. They said that since the Garden area had been fished, the catches in the rest of the bay had declined. The placing of the north-to-south line bounding the Marine Nature Reserve and the allocation of the area that would be closed to dredging and trawling was the central discussion point and it wasn't an easy decision.

There was an open meeting of the Island's main fishing co-operative, the Manx Fish Producers' Organisation, which gave the wider membership their say. Finally, a compromise was reached and we had the skeleton out-line of our Marine Nature Reserve, protecting all of the horse mussel reef we knew about, all of the seagrass and much of the maerl. The level of agreement was such that we were able to put out a joint press release between the Department of Environment, Food and Agriculture (DEFA) and the MFPO announcing the proposal made by the the fishing industry and DEFA's intention to take it forward. The MFPO at that time mainly represented trawl and dredge fishermen (trawls and dredges are sometimes known as mobile gear because they are pulled along behind a boat), with relatively few members who fished with pots (also known as static gear because they are deployed onto the seabed and stay there). We met with representatives of the pot fishermen with the map agreed by the trawl and dredge fishermen and talked about how we could protect the horse mussel reef from potting. From conservations like these we were able to suggest an area around the horse mussel reef that would also be protected from potting. Again, drawing and redrawing lines on maps, highlighting the best fishing areas and the most important habitats, made this possible.

After further discussions with pot fishermen, a zoning map for the Marine Nature Reserve was developed that offered a high level of protection for nature and was agreed by the people who made their living from the bay. At the time there wasn't consensus on the impact of potting on fragile seabed habitats, but more work that has recently been published confirms the importance of protecting special seabed habitats like horse mussel reef from potting. While potting has much less impact on the seabed than trawling or dredging, it can damage the structure of fragile habitats like reefs and it also impacts on the ecology of an area by removing key species like lobsters, so it can still have a significant impact on biodiversity. At that point I felt the most difficult negotiations were done – the commercial fishermen had fought for a compromise that left them with good access to fishing grounds and I'd worked hard to ensure the most important ecological features were going to be protected. We had agreed three zones – an inner Conservation Zone protecting the inshore maerl beds and kelp forest from trawling and dredging; a large Horse Mussel Zone protecting the horse mussel reef from trawling, dredging and potting; and an Eelgrass Zone protecting the eelgrass bed in the south of the bay from all fishing.

Fishing boats in Ramsey harbour.

Now we needed input from everyone else. We publicised the proposed zones that had been agreed by the commercial fishermen and we did a lot of engagement to get others involved. We wrote to all the major stakeholders and put out calls in the press to get a clearer idea of how people were currently using the bay and also any further information about the marine life and commercial species. We used a quick online survey as one of the options for people to respond but also met people face-to-face to talk through the options and implications.

The mood in Ramsey was really positive. From the first meeting of the Manx MNR project in Ramsey, where many people were concerned that they would not be able to have an MNR in Ramsey because of the sewage outlet, to the one where it was confirmed that Ramsey was going to be the site of the new MNR, enthusiasm for the Reserve only increased. We brought together all the input from the other stakeholders and began to finalise the zoning plan.

Before the final zoning was decided there were a couple more developments. Firstly, after all the negotiations about the positioning of the line between the fished area and the protected area, another idea evolved about the fished area. As the zones had developed, the protected areas formed a horseshoe shape around the centre of Ramsey Bay which was left open to fishing. After more discussions the idea of the fished area becoming a formal Fisheries Zone within the Marine Nature Reserve began to gain support. That way, there could be more control over how that area was fished and that could give additional protection not only to the nearby fragile habitats like maerl and horse mussel reef, but also to the fisheries. An agreement was reached that the Manx Fish Producers' Organisation would take on responsibility for managing the zone, while ensuring the 'ecological integrity' of the site. At the same time, we'd found new eelgrass meadows along the southern coast of the Marine Nature Reserve which fell inside the Fisheries Zone. It was agreed that they would be protected from dredging and trawling as a special Rocky Coast Zone. These five zones were finalised and we had our colourful zoning plan for a well-protected Marine Nature Reserve.

A local illustrator, John Caley, drew a wonderful map of the new Marine Nature Reserve for us to use on leaflets and signage and in the many talks I've done about the Reserve over the years, I've tried to bring that map to life. To me, Ramsey Bay is a cornucopia of colour and life, but you sometimes need a bit of guidance to discover its true wonder. There are the things that anyone can see as they explore the shore. The long expanse of beach that extends from the spindly iron legs of the Queen's Pier to Gob ny Rona can appear to be a featureless tract of sand, but there is so much there. Oystercatchers feed in the sand as the sea retreats, delving their long orange bills to seek out small bivalves like cockles. They are easily spooked and take flight to land a few metres further on to continue their foraging. The tide leaves behind a sprinkled edge of hairy heart-shaped sea potato shells – the fragile remnants of relatives of sea urchins which burrow in the sand and feed on detritus. Whatever time of year you walk along the beach, you'll find these in varying states of disintegration but very rarely still alive. The living sea potatoes are safe in their sandy burrows digesting the scavenged remains of other creatures. Razor shells are common in the sand towards the bottom of the shore and in the shallows. Their long shells sometimes litter the beach, uniform in their orange-brown colour, with bright white inside, some still paired and others single. After storms the bay reveals more secrets. Live king scallops can litter the low-tide mark, some still opening and closing their shells, others clamped shut and hopeful of being resubmerged before it is too late. Rare treats include a bunch of squid eggs, long, finger-like white sacks, each containing dozens of eggs and maybe as many as thirty, representing thousands of tiny cephalopod lives.

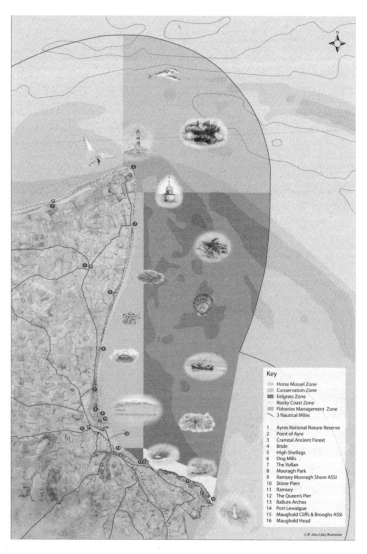

Illustration of Ramsey Bay Marine Nature Reserve
by John Caley.

In the spring, the shallow pools left behind in the sand as the tide goes out can be dotted with the small brown shapes of sea hares, another species of sea snail that thrives in the bay. They are much bigger than their cousins the nudibranchs, growing up to 20cm in length and they vary from dark brown and spotted to a bright red colour. Sea hares graze on seaweeds, including pink coralline seaweeds related to maerl, and reportedly the amount of red seaweed in the diet can influence their body colour, a bit like flamingoes and their pink shrimp prey. If you look more closely you can see that their red-brown surfaces are speckled with white. They have two sets of sensory tentacles, one at the front and one on the top of the head, and they crawl like terrestrial slugs along fronds of seaweed. The pools can seem infested with them, and then they disappear. There is evidence of this abundant species elsewhere too. In the mounds of seaweed at the top of the beach there are stringy tangles of eggs, pink like silly string and strewn across the strandline like the remnants of a mermaid party. They are the eggs of the sea hare.

The stretch of the beach between the Queen's Pier and the two stone piers which mark the entrance of the harbour is right in front of the centre of town and is the area most used by the community and visitors. In the summer the beach here can be full of families camped for the day, swimmers, paddle-boarders, kayakers and teenagers having sailing lessons in dinghies, safely within the piers. The worn stone slipway in front of the lighthouse is a gathering point. People sit with ice-creams, teenagers come down after school, hardened sea swimmers leave their towels on the smooth stones of the slip and brave the waves whatever the weather. In this shallow stretch between the piers, bottlenose dolphins occasionally come to feed, and at high tide, over the promenade wall, large silvery mullet can be seen with their upturned mouths feeding just below the surface.

Further out to sea, and not visible to the passer-by, there is a mosaic of ecosystems, distinct yet interconnected: kelp forests, maerl beds, brittlestar accumulations and horse mussel reefs, cobbles encrusted with exuberant blooms of plumose anemones, ever-shifting sand banks etched new with rippling ridges on every tide. In the south of the bay, just offshore from the bracken slopes and slate cliffs of the Maughold Brooghs, are bands of kelp forest, dense and waving in the current, interspersed with eelgrass meadows, clear and green. Further into the bay are writhing masses of brittlestars, wiry and skeletal versions of the more familiar common starfish, which form great heaps of living echinoderms that advance and retreat within the bay. They can happily exist in drifts of starfish metres thick, all sending up their pipe-cleaner arms to catch the passing plankton. They are particularly hated by fishermen, because when accidentally caught they fill the nets or dredges and can be too heavy to haul and empty, damaging equipment.

North of the stone piers, the gravelly seabed is transformed to pink by the scattering of maerl, just a sprinkling in places but elsewhere dense and full of life. Kelp and other seaweed species thrive within the maerl bed, hanging on the rocks and boulders. Young cod shelter in these inshore waters and juvenile shellfish like king scallops and queenies can settle. The water is clear and the maerl is dotted with burrowing sea anemones and bright red common sunstars, bigger than dinner plates and exuberant as Christmas decorations, with ten or more arms festooned with little white bunches of tubefect.

To the north the bay curves gently round and at the very northern tip of the Island is the Point of Ayre, with its distinctive lighthouse. A deep channel, the Ballacash Channel, runs between the point and the Ballacash Bank, and there are other shallower banks off the north of the Island – the Bahama Bank and the King William Bank. In the fast-running currents of the Ballacash Bank a never-ending buffet of plankton rushes past the filter-feeding horse mussels which have built reefs there. The seabed has been formed into mounds and valleys by the slow-growing masses of horse mussels, interspersed with soft corals.

On the shore towards the Point of Ayre, blue mussel beds create a habitat on the shore and provide a feeding ground for many species of bird which can smash the bright blue shells to access the nutritious animal inside. At Cranstal, where the sandy cliffs are not so high, the remains of an ancient forest were revealed after they were uncovered by a storm in 2014.

When we were going through the process of identifying sites that needed protection and places that would work well as Marine Nature Reserves, the needs of stakeholders were never far from our minds. We were sometimes questioned and to some extent challenged for the extensive stakeholder engagement we did.

I was so pleased with the way things turned out with the commercial fishermen. Initially they were very defensive and it was a struggle to engage them, but once we were able to build on their suggestion for designating Ramsey Bay and worked out the plans for a Fisheries Zone and their co-management of the area, it became a model for fisheries engagement in marine protected areas. There was a really positive article in the fishing industry newspaper, *Fishing News*, about how the Marine Nature Reserve had been developed in collaboration with the fishing industry and would benefit nature and fisheries. This article was in the same issue as a headline about UK marine protected areas destroying the fishing industry. Resistance from the fishing industry had always seemed like the biggest challenge to the project and I was pleased that we'd been able to work so well together to find a solution that brought so many benefits. However, I should have realised this had all been a bit too fortuitous. Things were about to get complicated again.

The black lugworm is a mysterious creature. Despite the widespread nature of lugworms and their ecological importance as the earthworms of the sandy shore, as well as their value to anglers who use them as bait, it was only in 1993 that it was discovered that the lugworms found around the British Isles were actually two separate species: the blow lug *Arenicola marina* and the black lug *Arenicola defodiens*. Lugworms create little tangled casts of sand on the beach, like tiny heaps of messily coiled rope. The two species of marine worm are virtually indistinguishable except to taxonomists and to anglers, who believe the black lugworm to be vastly superior as bait. But, interestingly, their casts can be used to tell them apart, as the black lug coils its excreted sandy poo more tidily, resulting in a neater worm cast.

In our zoning plan, Port Lewaigue was identified as the site to be most highly protected because of the presence of eelgrass, a diverse rocky shore and the important intertidal sand habitat which was home to lugworms, razor shells and other burrowing creatures. The zoning had progressed through a whole range of different consultations, from formal online surveys to one-to-one meetings with different sectors and individuals.

It was only when the zoning was officially announced that concerns emerged from some anglers. Anglers can be natural champions for healthy seas and are often very knowledgeable about the marine environment, but they are also very passionate about their hobby. Some of the anglers were really worried that the zoning plan would mean that they were going to lose access to an area they valued for bait digging, and particularly for the black lugworm. But what emerged from this and subsequent discussions was that the issue wasn't that we'd included the only black lugworm site in the highly protected Eelgrass Zone. It was that we'd included a black lugworm site within easy reach of a car park.

This is a great example of where marine science needs to be backed up with social science. Logically, there should be no reason why just one of a number of different black lugworm sites couldn't be protected, but we were forcing people to change their behaviour beyond what they found acceptable. While many of the anglers understood the wider benefits of the Marine Nature Reserve, what they were most interested in was how it was going to affect them and the recreational fishing they were passionate about. So, while commercial fishermen were persuaded of the value of keeping an important fishing area closed indefinitely, to protect spawning areas and allow build-up of breeding scallops, some anglers, who in many other ways had been champions of marine conservation, were more reluctant to give up access to their favourite bait-digging site.

Anglers can match commercial fishermen for their voice and influence, and once the anglers had decided they didn't agree with the zoning, things got complicated. At one point I was really concerned that 'lugwormgate' risked undermining the whole process and could have stopped the final Marine Nature Reserve regulations going through Tynwald. Eventually a compromise was reached. The area would remain highly protected, but it would not be no-take. There would be a temporary limited seasonal allowance for bait diggers to take lugworms and razor clams from the Port Lewaigue area. This would be permitted for six months in the winter (October to March) and then for the rest of the year the site would be no-take. I wasn't happy, because the no-take zone was already so small. At the same time, I was concerned that this issue could put a stop to the whole thing, so I was very relieved that a solution had been found.

Let me describe how the Ramsey Bay Marine Nature Reserve looked in the end. From the top of Barrule the Marine Nature Reserve is spread before you almost to its full extent but all you can see is sea — you have to use your imagination about the changing topography beneath.

From the Point of Ayre in the north round to Maughold
Head in the east, the MNR extends three miles from shore
and protects around 95 square kilometres of seabed (around
9500 hectares, which is 9500 football pitches or Trafalgar
Squares). It extends to three nautical miles because the Isle
of Man has fuller control over inshore waters. The Isle of
Man Government owns the territorial sea out to twelve
nautical miles but more consultation and agreement from
our neighbours is needed for measures brought in outside
the three-mile limit. The whole of the bay is protected by
secondary legislation under the Wildlife Act 1990 from a
whole variety of impacts; special permission is required
for any development to go ahead in the MNR. The inner
waters of the bay from south of the Queen's Pier and
north to beyond the high sandy cliffs of the Shellags are
protected as a Conservation Zone. No trawling or dredging is allowed in this area, to protect the precious pink
maerl beds and the kelp forests, but setting pots (mainly
for lobster) is permitted. The Conservation Zone includes
a significant part of what the fishermen call the Garden,
which they highlighted as being particularly important for
the juvenile king scallops: the diverse, structurally complex
seabed that provides a settling place for those vulnerable
little baby scallops. The scallops spend their first month or
so as part of the plankton, then when they are still tiny they
attach themselves to seabed plants and animals (especially
the plant-like animals like hydroids and bryozoans, whose
colonies form fragile branching structures that can look
like ferns, bare trees or dried foliage) until they are the size
of a lentil when they detach and make their permanent
home snuggled into the sandy seabed.

To the east of the Point of Ayre is the Horse Mussel Zone (you may be able to tell that these zones were given working titles that somehow stuck and got written into legislation). That protects the horse mussel reef that thrives in the currents of the Ballacash Channel from trawling and dredging, and also from potting. The only commercial fishing that can take place in the zone is line fishing and, given the strong currents and sometimes difficult conditions in this area, the impact of that is thought to be quite minimal so I would consider this zone 'highly protected'. South of the Horse Mussel Zone and adjacent to the Conservation Zone is the Fisheries Management Zone. This makes up half of the total area of the MNR and is the zone which is co-managed by the fishermen of the Manx Fish Producers' Organisation and the Department of Environment, Food and Agriculture. In the surveys that have been done in the area since the MNR was finalised, additional areas of horse mussel reef and maerl bed have been found in this zone and the fishermen have undertaken to fish the area without impacting on these habitats. Their fishing for king scallops is confined to a small proportion of the Fisheries Management Zone (at the time of writing less than 10 per cent) leaving the rest of the area protected year-round as an effective part of the MNR.

In the south-west corner of the bay, between the Ballure Arches and Gob ny Rona, is the Eelgrass Zone. This is where eelgrass was originally found and is the most highly protected zone, the only extraction of marine life permitted being seasonal bait digging from October to March. The much more extensive eelgrass beds with their clouds of fish and grazing top shells, between Port Lewaigue and

Stack Mooar, were discovered subsequent to the initial zoning and are protected in the Rocky Coast Zone, along with the adjacent shallow kelp forests.

Around the edge of the MNR there are now colourful information boards which Dr Lara Howe at the Manx Wildlife Trust designed on DEFA's behalf using John Caley's beautiful illustrations, so at many popular access spots you can orientate yourself in the Marine Nature Reserve and learn about the marine life and its protection.

Ramsey from the north.

The Sulby river which flows into Ramsey Bay is one of the biggest on the Island, and at full flow it feels like a substantial river. Most of the other rivers on the Isle of Man are little more than streams. There is an old stone bridge at the top of the harbour. It joins Ramsey town centre and south Ramsey with north Ramsey. Look right as you're crossing it and you see the harbour, a mix of boats that look like they've been there for ever, and newer yachts and fishing boats, then beyond is the swing bridge that can open to let larger vessels out. The shipyard is still operating after more than 160 years and there is usually a fishing boat or another vessel up on the slip having work done, and others tied up alongside waiting for their turn. The slipway is wide and can accommodate big commercial fishing vessels and even the cargo vessels that operate out of Ramsey that are over forty metres long and completely fill the slip. The oldest active sailing ship in the world, the *Star of India*, was built in Ramsey in 1863 and while she is now part of a museum, she still sails out of San Diego from time to time.

If you look to your left as you walk out of Ramsey you see the estuary of the Sulby and the Poyll Dooey saltmarsh. There is always some sort of waterfowl in the area. In October there can be hundreds of Canada geese, assembling for migration. They patrol up and down the river in large groups and dozens of them nestle and feed and interact on the tufts of saltmarsh that fringe the river. Occasionally you can spot, so white it looks artificial, the little egret with its dark, watchful eye. It wades and feeds with its long bill from high up the river in the saltmarsh, down through the muds of the harbour and out onto the sandy shore. I've seen it for a few consecutive years now and like to think it is the same one, but maybe not. It is a species that is thought to be becoming more common around Irish Sea coasts with climate change.

There are around a dozen swans that frequent the harbour too. Their guardian is a retired pot fisherman who makes sure they are not troubled. He has fished in the bay for decades and was a wonderful source of information on the habitats and currents when we were developing the Reserve. On a gravelly island that supports the swing bridge that connects north and south Ramsey, a pair of oystercatchers often make their nest. It is a pebbly, fort-like construction, and it is always perilously close to the high-tide mark. I've not seen the young but the pair return year after year to this unusual nesting place, though they are vulnerable to very high spring tides when the little island under the bridge can completely disappear.

Poyll Dooey is such a special place. There is very little saltmarsh on the Isle of Man and Poyll Dooey is probably the most extensive continuous area. There is a small area at Cornaa, about five miles down the coast from Ramsey and on the Langness peninsula saltmarsh forms part of the Area of Special Scientific Interest. Tufts of saltmarsh grasses and other hardy, salt-loving plants are interspersed with surprisingly deep pools. In the early summer carpets of thrift (sea pink) cover the higher reaches of the hardy saltmarsh edges. The pools look clear when undisturbed but have layer upon layer of mud beneath the water. They are alive with little invertebrates that you can see stirring at the edges of the pools. When they froze one winter, we realised they were also full of small fish – little speckled gobies and the juveniles of other species. The geese and ducks and waders that frequent the saltmarsh are feeding on these mud-loving creatures and saltmarsh is a very rich and productive habitat.

At low tide when the river is low there is an expanse of estuarine mud, rich and gloopy and full of good things for wading birds like redshanks and oystercatchers to eat. At high tide and when the river is full after rains (in spate), the water submerges much of the saltmarsh and laps over the grassy edges of the paths. It flows seaward at pace.

The Sulby is a salmon river, though I've never seen them myself. It is also home to a good population of European eels, which while they are also known as common eels have become increasingly endangered in recent decades. A visiting MSc student set traps to study and release the eels and I helped him empty the traps, struggling farcically with the slimy, writhing creatures. Eels are really suffering throughout Europe, where they are now categorised as critically endangered, and our healthy population in the Isle of Man needs active protection. Eels in continental Europe have been lost to fishing, particularly for young eels which are a delicacy, and also loss of their habitat. It is hard to believe that the mud-colour, earthy-smelling eels that can be seen along the Sulby river have made that astounding migration to the Sargasso Sea on the other side of the Atlantic, before returning to their home river. Such a dull creature and such a glamorous lifestyle.

Saltmarsh is a blue carbon habitat that can store vast quantities of carbon, so if we can restore and extend the areas of this habitat we remove carbon dioxide from the atmosphere and help to mitigate climate change. Conversely, if we destroy, degrade or pollute the habitat, this can lead to the release of greenhouse gases, making things worse. While recognition of the essential role that habitats like saltmarshes play in our urgent efforts to curb climate change is increasing internationally, at the same time these habitats are being encroached on by development and eroded and degraded through poor management. A message that came clearly from the latest United Nations Framework on Climate Change Conference of the Parties in Glasgow (COP26) was that when it comes to natural stores of carbon, our first priority must be to save what we have. Focusing on restoration and replanting while simultaneously letting our precious carbon hotspots be lost is often worse than useless.

The estuarine habitats of Ramsey harbour and saltmarsh further up the river at Poyll Dooey aren't protected at the moment. In 2010 their importance was recognised and they were protected as an Area of Special Scientific Interest, but the designation was contentious and was overturned later that year, leaving the area unprotected. Because of this controversy, although the estuary and saltmarsh are essential parts of the Ramsey Bay ecosystem and inextricably connected, they were not included in the Marine Nature Reserve designation. Development is creeping closer on the Poyll Dooey Nature Reserve and saltmarsh and even the Marine Nature Reserve is not safe from development, but we lose these natural carbon stores and flood defences at our peril.

All over the world people are understanding the importance of integrated coastal management, or ridge-to-reef conservation as it's known in more tropical climes. There are no boundaries in nature between ocean and land, freshwater and salt. The salmon and eels move between river and ocean, the seabirds feed in the estuary and on the shore, and fish like plaice and mullet can move far up the estuary into the river. The health of Ramsey Bay MNR depends on the health of the river that feeds into it and the estuary and saltmarsh. The ecology of many species depends on movement between sea and river, either their own or the movement of nutrients or prey species. A good example of the interconnectivity of sea and river is the sea lamprey. These primitive fish are often found hanging on to the sides of basking sharks far out to sea. Some sharks will have five or six of them. Attached to basking sharks, they may cover thousands of kilometres at sea, crossing the Atlantic Ocean and beyond. They are more commonly found as parasites on smaller fish like salmon, cod and haddock. But for the beginning and end of their life cycle they live independently and need clean rivers and freshwater habitats. Many species have complex ecological requirements and we need to ensure that we are protecting the wide range of habitats to sustain the widest diversity of species.

In 2010, aged thirty-seven and having been single for two years since a doomed long-distance relationship had ended, I had driven north to Ramsey to spend Christmas with my parents. For as long as I can remember we've spent Christmas Eve at a small gathering organised by family friends. What had been fun as a child became something of an obligation as a teenager, something to be endured before heading off to the busy pubs on the harbour. I had been to the gathering in the years when I'd been living abroad and returned home just in time for Christmas.

That year I was catching up with my parents' friends, many of whom were also my old teachers, and their children, my contemporaries, most of whom had left the Island to go to university and unlike me not returned, when Rob came to sit next to me and we got chatting. I'd known Rob since the early Christmas Eve gatherings when we were both at junior school. Most years he'd be there with his latest girlfriend and I was usually there without a boyfriend, usually because I was single or because I was just back for Christmas and whoever I had been seeing hadn't come with me. His sister was visiting from Scotland with her husband and they'd all been out sledging earlier in the day and were all full of that excitement. Rob was thirty-eight and had been single for a year or so too. We had never been interested in each other at school and had moved in completely different circles, but at that cosy Christmas Eve gathering eating trifle heavily laced with sherry, we found lots to talk about. And so, in homage to Bridget Jones, I found my future husband at a Christmas Eve gathering that my mother had cajoled me into going to. Neither of us was wearing a Christmas jumper, but we may as well have been. Our first date was a walk down the steep winding paths of Dhoon Glen where the recent snow had flattened down the ferns and other vegetation and everything seemed to drip down towards the beach. On the beach we ate mince pies and drank coffee with brandy. Between Christmas and New Year we went for a wintry walk every day and on New Year's Eve, which I'd planned to spend back at home in Port Erin, he lured me to his house with the promise of showing me his dried bat collection (Rob is a builder specialising in the conservation of historic buildings and has spent a lot of time on or inside church roofs) – a biologist is easily tempted by the promise of dead wildlife. While Rob's work seems a world away from mine, there are many parallels. Conserving historic buildings using traditional techniques is another way we can enrich what we pass on to future generations. Like nature conservation, building conservation is not always supported or valued as much as it should be. Rob's love of the Island's heritage and his time spent in farmyards and castles and churches has also informed his other work – as a sculptor. Through reforming and reshaping abandoned steel he creates rebalanced forms.

There was something else we had in common. Both of us had been told a tragic story as a child that had stuck with us into adulthood. It was my grandfather who had told me the story. It dated from 1918 when he was a little boy, the youngest of ten children and living in a little croft up at Ronague in the hills of the south of the Island. He went to Arbory School and while he was there, a terrible tragedy occurred which he would never forget. One lunchtime two twelve-year-old girls in his class, Isabel and Essie, were playing by the stream in the school grounds and found some hemlock plants. For some reason they thought the plants (which were said to resemble parsnips) were edible and they both tried some. On their way back to school they began to feel ill and Essie collapsed. Their parents were sent for. Essie deteriorated rapidly and died shortly afterwards. Isabel was taken back to the family farm and made to drink large volumes of milk, fresh from the cow which made her very sick. She must have vomited up the hemlock root and she went on to make a full recovery. Hemlock water dropwort, as it is now known, is one of the most toxic plants in the British Isles and even a tiny amount of the root can cause terrible convulsions and death. The image of those two girls and their pinafore dresses and bows in their long hair was always vivid in my imagination. The lesson from the tale, about not eating anything you couldn't identify with certainty, stuck with me, as did the miracle survival of Isabel whose family knew what to do and did it straight away. If it hadn't been for those quick-thinking parents and an obliging cow, my son wouldn't be here today. Rob's Nana Isabel died long before we got together, so I never heard the story direct from her, but we've combined the family stories and Dylan has heard it more than once and will be able to hand it down, along with a healthy respect for toxic plants.

8

Success

'She returns to the deep of the sea
Who was flung for a little space
Upon the shores of the world. She has won free
Of life's heavy dream, and the peace of Manannan
Wraps her again.'

Mona Douglas, 'Teeval of the Sea'

It is a Sunday in July 2011 when we go searching for more eelgrass in Ramsey Bay. I'm part of the small team of divers. We don't have the necessary set-up for me to dive for work, so the diving I do to inform my work is done recreationally or as a volunteer Seasearch diver with Tony Glen and his fellow Seasearchers. The first dive I do is with Geoff, a really keen and experienced diver with a strong interest in the environment. I am really excited about doing this dive. I've been excited about the Ramsey seagrass since I first heard about it and found little clumps on the beach by the wrecked trawler years before. It was not long after I'd moved back to the Island and I was walking on the beach with my dad when I spotted, bright green among the glossy brown tangle of wrack, chunks of very fresh-looking grass held together by tangled webs of roots. At the time I took a lot of photos and tried to find out more. I knew there was eelgrass in a sheltered gulley off Langness but I hadn't heard about it growing in Ramsey Bay. I was keen to find out more.

We are diving from Discover Diving's boat, the *Endeavour*. It is a purpose-built dive boat which even has a lift on the back to haul you into the boat – much easier than flinging yourself over the side of an inflatable boat. We have a plan to drop divers in right along the coast from Maughold Head round to Port-e-Vullen. We're diving first under Maughold Brooghs, the grassy slopes that end in steeper, rocky, slate cliffs entering the sea. We know that eelgrass is very particular about the conditions it grows in. It isn't able to withstand exposure to the full brunt of Irish Sea storms and it needs a good amount of light, so dense beds only tend to be found in a particular type of sheltered shallow water.

We are dropped off and descend into nine metres of water. There is a little fuzz of plankton so the visibility isn't perfect. We swim through some kelp and within a couple of minutes of the start of the dive we've hit eelgrass. It's patchy but undeniably meadow-like and hung with darting curtains of orange two-spot gobies picking at plankton from the water column. I breathe out and sink down in among the blades of grass, also fuzzy with the epiphytic algae growing on them. A little patch of sandy seabed peels itself loose and flurries into the cover of the grass – a juvenile flatfish of some sort.

I am smiling madly underwater and grin at my dive

buddy. We lay out the fifty-metre measuring tape and start our survey. We estimate the cover of eelgrass, the proportion of the seabed over which eelgrass is growing. It gets as high as 80 per cent on this dive and we also note down the abundance of other plants and animals and the seabed type: sand, gravel and so on. It is straightforward science and it is enough to inform future management and help us understand what is there and how it can be protected.

Seasearch diver on the first seagrass dive off Maughold.

One of the things that never fails to surprise me about Manx waters is the abundance and diversity of anemones. There are more than seventy species of sea anemone known from the waters of the British Isles, although before I returned to work on the Isle of Man I could probably have named only a couple of them. Many of the species are cryptic, buried in sediment or well camouflaged and many are very difficult to tell apart unless you are an expert.

In the eelgrass beds below the brooghs there are more burrowing anemones than I've ever seen before. They have a short-tentacled chrysanthemum centre surrounded by a wide-eyed halo of much longer translucent tentacles. Unlike the beadlet anemones on the shore, this type of anemone doesn't need to be attached to a hard surface. Instead, it has its own felty tube and can retract its whole body back into the tube to escape predation.

Early on in the dive I spot one of our most vibrant fish. A male dragonet, completely still on the seabed, sitting on its splayed pectoral fins, gold- and sapphire-jewelled and undeniably dragon-like. The females can have paler blue patterning but are not as striking as the males (this is often the way with fish). Tiny and disgruntled-looking (the comedy sad faces of gobies always remind me a little of Muppets), painted gobies try to fade into the sandy seabed. These little scavengers seem to like divers, following their trail of inadvertently swirled-up seabed to eat small worms and shrimps. A spotted catshark (remember, the fish formerly known as dogfish) curves off into the cover of eelgrass. At the very end of the dive, in moderate eelgrass cover sits a one-clawed lobster, dark bodied with Biro-blue legs. I wonder what happened to the other claw. There are lobster pots in the area so it could have lost a claw escaping a pot or being returned to the sea because it was too small. Or, it could have lost it to a predator. I wasn't expecting to see a lobster out in the open and take photos, excited. When we surface, I am brimming with delight – the eelgrass is here. It was here all the time, when

I walked along that stretch of coast with my parents as a child.

After our surface interval drinking tea and talking fish and looking things up in the boat copies of identification books, Geoff and I go back in. This time we're just south of Port-e-Vullen, north of our previous dive. Port-e-Vullen is a favourite beach of mine and where we often went to swim and rockpool as children. Here the eelgrass is not so lush, but there is eelgrass in most of the five-metre sections of our transect all the same. On this dive I spot the roughly circular slight indentation in the sandy gravel that is a telltale sign of the hastily buried king scallop just below the surface. Fixed to one blade of eelgrass is the Medusa-like mass of the snakelocks anemone. The mauve-grey tentacles swish with the movement of the water awaiting the capture of some tiny passing invertebrate. And later we see the large, sprawled orange form of a common starfish. More striking is the red-purple, almost coral-like form of a bloody Henry starfish.

Port-e-Vullen beach.

In December 2011 we finally got the Marine Nature Reserve designated. It was a wonderful feeling when the legislation was approved by Tynwald, the Isle of Man's 1000-year-old parliament. Phil Gawne was the minister at the time and took the legislation to Tynwald.

On 17 January 2012 the full by-laws were laid before Tynwald. They had been amended from the previous version to temporarily allow seasonal bait digging in the previously no-take Eelgrass Zone.

The Marine Nature Reserve was in place and Ramsey Bay was finally protected. As with any busy job there is never much time to celebrate a success because you are already busy with the next thing. In 2012 the fishermen opted to keep the Fisheries Management Zone closed for the year. The area was patrolled by the fisheries protection vessel the *Barrule* and the movements of fishing vessels could be monitored remotely using the satellite monitoring devices that all larger fishing vessels are required to carry. There were some teething troubles as people got used to the regulations. There were reports of illegal dredging at night and of divers illegally taking scallops, but there were few problems and the MNR became an accepted part of Ramsey life.

Rob and I got married in August 2012 in the registry office at Castle Rushen – one of the best-preserved medieval castles in the British Isles – and then had a very sea-themed reception at the Sound Café, which looks out over the seal hotspot of Kitterland and the wonders of the Calf of Man. Our wedding photographs were taken at low tide with plenty of seaweed and rockpools visible behind the guests (which made me very happy). Pete, who had hosted the Christmas Eve party where we met, made us an amazing fish-themed wedding cake. I was thirty-nine and Rob was forty and as so many of our friends were bringing children, I wanted to make them welcome at the wedding. I had dropped off a big box of cuddly fish, hermit crabs and other sea-themed soft toys (marine education props) for the children to play with at the reception but someone at the venue had thought they were to decorate the room so when we got there after the wedding there were cuddly penguins, fish puppets and plush puffins strategically placed all around the room. It wasn't exactly what I had planned but it seemed somehow very appropriate.

In November 2012 I found out I was pregnant. We were both a little bit amazed but delighted.

I like to think that the Marine Nature Reserve played an important part in Dylan's birth. I had a good pregnancy. I kept up regular swimming right until I gave birth and I didn't really have any problems, despite being forty at the time. The only time when I felt my age became an issue was when I went over my due date and the guidance is to induce older mums. I had been going to a chiropractor for some pelvic girdle pain and she was a great proponent of natural birth and not a fan of inductions, and I was really keen to avoid a highly medicalised birth. I turned down two opportunities to be induced, one on my due date and one the week after, and tried all the recommended 'natural' approaches to induce labour, including drinking copious quantities of raspberry leaf tea and eating lots of pineapple. But on the tenth day after my due date I was beginning to get desperate. I was enormous by then. During those ten days I seemed to have ballooned to unimaginable size. On the Saturday afternoon, ten days overdue, I had an overwhelming compulsion to go for a long hilly walk. I told Rob I was going and said it was up to him whether he came with me or not. Despite being much less risk-averse than I normally am, even he thought he should accompany an enormously overdue woman staggering along the coastal path from Port-e-Vullen up to Maughold Head. It is probably my best-loved walk. It starts just up the road from Port-e-Vullen beach, one of my favourites for swimming, and takes you along the Maughold Brooghs where I can always now envisage the inshore band of eelgrass that we discovered on the dives in 2011, and then the outer band of kelp. I was driven forward with a superhuman compulsion to walk briskly and climb steep hills and when I look back at the photos now I don't know how I did it. Just before the first climb on the walk you can stand at the end of a sheer cliff and look down on Stack Mooar, a tiny rocky islet separated from the brooghs by maybe ten metres of water. There are two wind-twisted old Scots pines at the bottom of the hill and we have a family tradition from when I was very young to stop and give the broad trunk of the tree nearest the path a hug. This time it had to be a sideways hug before starting the climb up the grassy path through the bracken. But it felt so good to be putting one walking-booted foot in front of another and making it to the funny little bus shelter that looks down over Maughold and back over Ramsey Bay Marine Nature Reserve. The risk of having to be rescued by the coastguard was averted on the way back as we took the loop path that returned us to the car by the road. We went home and Rob cooked a tomato pasta which I remember particularly enjoying and then by the time I went to bed at ten p.m. my labour had started.

On the Sunday my labour continued and during the day I had a vomiting labour, which I'd never even heard of, but every time I had a contraction I threw up. I spent a lot of time pacing around the garden until we decided it was time to head to hospital, me clutching an ice-cream tub to be sick in. After swimming all through my pregnancy I was really keen to use the birthing pool. When I went into active labour at about nine p.m. I went into a warm pool in a twilit room with stars on the ceiling. I had a lovely few hours on gas and air, wallowing around in the pool like a misshapen beluga whale. Then during one of the routine monitoring sessions, they picked up that the baby was in distress and I was whipped out of my watery haven into the delivery suite next door. Everything happened very quickly and next thing I'd had an epidural and a forceps delivery. There was an appliquéd picture of a coral reef on the wall of the delivery suite though, and I felt that was appropriate, in the absence of actual water.

As a biologist I found the whole process of pregnancy and birth fascinating. While I was pregnant I read a brilliant book about the placenta, so I was very keen to keep mine. I did have plans to try cooking it but I forgot to bring the cool box and it sat in a plastic bag on a hot August day for slightly longer than I would have liked, so we froze it and, after I'd dissected the livery mass, we buried it under a new apple tree in our garden.

Because of the complications at birth, Dylan had swal-lowed some meconium (like the vomiting labour this was another thing I hadn't been prepared for – meconium is a newborn baby's first poo and can be released during a complicated birth) and developed a fever the day after he was born. We were still in hospital so he was taken straight over to neonatal intensive care and fitted with an intra-venous drip for antibiotics and a feeding tube. I honestly thought that once I'd got past the later weeks of pregnancy I didn't need to worry about neonatal intensive care, so I wasn't really prepared for the week that Dylan spent in a little incubator. But the nurses on the unit couldn't have been more lovely and I never had any doubt that he was in the best possible hands. Because there was space, I was able to stay on in a side ward and run backwards and forwards between the ward and neonatal intensive care to either attempt to breastfeed Dylan or sit connected up to the pumping machine so I could produce breast milk that could go into his feeding tube. It was all a bit traumatic, but after a week he was fine and we could come home.

We are out on the Maughold Brooghs. I have Dylan in a little baby carrier on my front. He is snuggled into my chest and I am fretting about him suffocating. It is a bright day with a bit of a breeze and I am just so happy to be out in the fresh air with Dylan and Rob. I walk carefully, afraid that I will fall and crush him. I'm worrying about his temperature too. Is he getting too hot bundled so close to me?

But gradually, as we walk, I let go and relax into the sea and the bracken slopes. It is only just over two weeks since

I did this walk before, laden with my huge bump, crazed with the need to climb hills and jog-walk down slopes. Now that he is outside, Dylan seems so tiny. All the bulk for such a little thing.

We reach the clump of Scots pines, bowed by the wind into hooked claws on the edge of the cliff. This is where we always stopped to hug the scaly bulk of the trunks of these resilient trees. Now I put down my waterproof and gently lay Dylan out. His proximity to the grass under the trees seems so alien. For over a week he's been in an incubator, without a leaf or an ant in sight.

I'm so relieved that he is breathing the sea air. I've left the neonatal intensive care promising not to rely on breastfeeding which has been challenging. The head nurse emphasised that it was essential that he got the extra input from formula milk. Under the trees I try to breastfeed, and then I give him the bottle I've brought as well. Two young women walk past and notice how tiny he is, how recognisably newborn and they coo as they say hello, and already I feel guilty that I'm giving him formula from a plastic bottle.

A photo from that day shows me in a red top which I remember being a special breastfeeding-adapted top that was a favourite for a long time. Dylan's skin looks red and his eyes, unusually, are closed. In the background is the sea and the rock, a little triangle islet with some small patches of grass, but mainly just jagged slate.

My year of maternity leave also gave me the chance to feel more a part of the Ramsey community than I had for years. My usual walk took me down along the harbourside, looking over the edge of the harbour wall onto the decks of little pleasure fishing boats, wooden sailing ships, refurbished lifeboats and then the rows of trawlers and dredgers that fish for queen and king scallops. I had stepped away from the management of the Marine Nature Reserve, but I was able to keep an eye on it as I strode along the promenade with the pram, stopping at each opening down onto the beach to show Dylan the sea, or watching the fishing boats coming and going in the harbour.

As agreed when we developed the Marine Nature Reserve zones, only very carefully controlled fishing of the Fisheries Management Zone was allowed. Various ways of doing this were discussed and it was a challenge to find the right solution – this was a completely new way of doing things. A core principle was that fishermen would have control over the fisheries zone while being committed to maintaining the ecological integrity of the site. This was obviously open to interpretation, but encompassed both the health of the king scallop population and the protection of the seabed habitats so important to support the ecosystem. To ensure the ecological integrity, decisions on management needed to be based on good science.

The first year the zones were in place, the science was led by DEFA working with the Bangor University scientists and the fishermen. We worked with the Manx Fish Producers' Organisation to design the surveys but it was undoubtedly more of a scientific survey than a fisheries survey.

The first year that the fishermen fished in Ramsey Bay was 2013, when I was on maternity leave. That year each fishing boat was given a quota to fish within a specified area and a specified period of time in December. Many of the boats decided to pool their quotas, with two, three or even four vessels working together to fish from one boat and then divide the income from the catch. This made for a super-efficient approach to fishing. Instead of three individual boats setting out to their favoured grounds based on their years of experience and an element of good luck, in the tightly regulated Fisheries Management Zone the fishermen knew exactly where the high concentrations of scallops were. Informed by the scientific survey, they could sail a few hundred metres from the harbour (in the case of Ramsey fishing boats), fish in the high densities and be finished within a few hours. This made for not only minimal impact on the seabed habitats of the bay and the ecosystems they sustain but also seafood with a remarkably low carbon footprint. Dr Isobel Bloor from Bangor University led a study of the fuel use per kilo of scallop caught and found that the Ramsey Bay scallops, particularly those caught that first year, were among some of the lowest-carbon seafood in the world. She went on to make comparisons with other animal protein and found that Ramsey Bay scallops were among the lowest-carbon sources of protein to have been studied. This comes with the caveat that many extremely low carbon fisheries just haven't been studied to that extent. I know that the sea-grass fishery I studied for my PhD must have had a very low carbon footprint – no fossil fuel engines, no fancy boats, just old sail-powered vessels – but in terms of more industrialised fisheries and meat production the Ramsey scallops come out very well.

Over a few years, the approach to managing the Fisheries Management Zone moved away from DEFA doing the science and providing options for management, to the fishermen doing the surveys themselves, with help from the Bangor University scientists and coming up with their own management plan. This has been helped by technology – instead of printed measuring boards and scribbling down the scallop measurements and other information on plastic boards or waterproof paper, the new boards are electronic, and record the measurements of the scallops in a format that can then be emailed back to the fishermen. The boards are designed and made in New Zealand and as well as helping fisheries scientists they are giving fishermen the tools to do their own science and perhaps most importantly, have the option to make every fishing trip a research opportunity.

Each year the fishermen have caught more scallops within the Fisheries Management Zone, usually fishing in December when they can get the highest prices in the run-up to Christmas. Studies by the Bangor University scientists, using the satellite tracking information from the fishing vessels (and onboard GPS as well), have shown that the footprint of the fishing effort is limited to well under 10 per cent of the area of the Fisheries Management Zone. Large areas of horse mussel reef, brittlestar beds, kelp and maerl are not fished at all from one year to the next, and so they act like a highly protected part of the Marine Nature Reserve.

One sure sign that a marine protected area is working well is when you see fishing boats fishing right up to its boundary, or 'fishing the line'. As concentrations of fish or shellfish build up inside the MPA, they begin to move out in two different ways. In the case of scallops, with their little bursts of energy they can move a few metres in a day, so those near the edges of the MPA can gradually end up moving out into the fished area in the course of their daily movement. While king scallops spend most of their time sitting quietly on the seabed filtering out plankton, the approach of a predator like a common starfish can lead to one of those exhausting little flurries of activity that could see them moving tens of metres.

The other way that scallops and many other marine animals can move out of the protected area and boost numbers in fished areas is as plankton. Many marine animals spend their first few days, weeks or even months as part of the plankton. They may first be released as eggs which spend time floating around on currents, and then when they hatch the larval stages can also spend time floating about, although perhaps with a bit more control over where they are going. Larval stages can also look very different from adult creatures. While larval scallops are not instantly recognisable as scallops, they do look like tiny shells (or bivalves – two-shelled molluscs); the larvae of the brown or edible crabs that are fished for in Manx waters look like spiky little aliens. It would be difficult to guess what species they are (I remember being completely foxed when I saw my first crab larvae in light traps we were using to study fish larvae in the Caribbean).

In what seemed like an instant, I was back at work, which presented its own challenges. I went back to work full-time when Dylan was ten and a half months old, but with flexibility around working from home some days and having time with Dylan other days during the day and then catching up in the evenings.

I know a lot of women confess to finding the early months and years of motherhood hard going but I loved my time with Dylan while he was a baby. We spent lots of time outdoors, first on my daily marches with the pram along the promenade looking out over the Marine Nature Reserve, and then as Dylan got bigger with him in a rucksack-style baby carrier walking in the hills above Ramsey and looking back down over the whole of the bay from the top of Lhergy Frissel, and sitting in front of the Albert Tower to have a drink from my water bottle and feed Dylan an oat bar. I loved talking to his bright little face behind me on my back. Pointing out the unfurling beech leaves or the clumps of blue bells in the woods above Ramsey, or the swans gliding out into the bay like luxury yachts. When he was just ten weeks old we went to Marseille so I could attend the International Marine Protected Areas Congress, a global MPA meeting which I'd previously been able to attend in Washington DC in 2009. I was presenting a poster and had applied to go before I knew I was pregnant. It was surprisingly easy to travel with such a young baby, and it was so inspiring to be able to emerge from the cocoon of maternity leave in Ramsey and be among the leading MPA scientists and advocates from around the world all gathered in one place. I do have enduring memories though of sitting in our hotel bathroom pumping breast milk in the middle of the night to leave with Rob for emergencies, and of literally running up and down the Marseille quayside at lunchtime to feed Dylan back at the hotel (we tried street cafés and park benches nearer the venue but he was too distracted with all the colour and excitement around him to feed quickly). Rob had a great time sitting outside quayside bars, with Dylan in the buggy next to him, watching the world go by.

Back home and wrapped up against the winter weather, I took Dylan to properly explore the south of the Island, introducing him to Spaldrick beach, holding him up to look into the rockpool on Betsy Donnag and showing him handfuls of storm-cast seaweed, full of colours and diverse foliage shapes, from the daintiest skeletons of coralline algae to the rubbery bulk of big kelp stipes, his chubby hands reaching out to feel the slippery surface. I was lucky to have met a lovely group of local mums through going to pregnancy yoga and then to an aquanatal group for pregnant women and we met weekly for coffee and shared all the usual angst first on sleeping and feeding and then on the challenges and complications of childcare as, one by one, we returned to work. I appreciated living near to my mum and dad and could pop round for lunch so they could dote on Dylan, and Rob's parents were close to my daily pram march route so I could pop in there sometimes too.

I am out on the fisheries protection vessel *Barrule*, which also doubles as our research vessel. It's my first trip out since returning from maternity leave and fieldwork is presenting some new challenges. I've been catching up on the news at sea and hearing the enforcement officers' views on how the latest fishery management measures are working out and their thoughts on the marine conservation work. I've had to excuse myself and head below to the loo.

As soon as I lock the door, the vessel lurches and I stumble. With difficulty I wriggle out of my yellow oil-skin smock that smells of sea and tarpaulins and struggle to unclip the matching dungarees. I peel off a jumper, a thermal top, a T-shirt and finally undo my bra. I get some initial relief. I catch a glimpse of myself in the small mirror and have to look again. I look like I've been Photoshopped.

I do some calculations. I usually fed Dylan around 6.30 a.m. but I left home before that this morning, when he was still asleep. So the last time I fed him was around three a.m. We were supposed to be doing a short day at sea so I was expecting to be able to pick him up from Mum and Dad's around five. It's now gone eight, and we aren't due back into port until eleven at the earliest – twenty hours lactating at sea like a grey seal who's lost her pup.

I've been working out on deck all day, steadying the grab as it comes in, sieving the samples of fine red worms, delicate shrimps with translucent bodies and the occasional larger bivalve, and dividing out the dripping sand and mud into labelled foil takeaway containers. I'm helping a colleague with his sampling and we have to finish today, because the boat goes onto the shipyard slip tomorrow. The grab hadn't been working properly early on which had set us back hours.

We'd been stowing the gear ready to steam round to the offshore site at Targets when one of my colleagues had popped his head out of the bridge: 'Change of plan, lads, we're going to work through. That OK with you Doc?'

This is my first day back at sea and I answer in an instant, 'Sure, that's fine.'

Five hours later and I'm struggling to keep my balance in the tiny windowless toilet as I try to hand-express. I've never done this before and regret not paying more attention at the La Leche League meetings now. It doesn't work and the attempt is agony. The skin of my breasts is straining and my nipples are burning. I try to fan them with my hands, hoping the cool air might help. I run some tissue under the pump-operated tap and make little pads and apply them gently. Wetting toilet paper always seems to be such an act of desperation. In all those books and meetings and earnest conversations over cups of nursing tea and obligatory baked goods, nobody ever told me how to deal with anything like this. I want to Google it, but the computer's right next to the skipper, and it's being used for putting in the data. I think of texting the queen bee nursing guru mummy who runs the coffee mornings but where would I start? I try to channel my most capable friend, but it is hard to imagine her, Boden-clad and eternally organised, finding herself in a situation like this.

Instead, I compose an imaginary Mayday: 'FPV *Barrule*. 8 miles south-south-west of Douglas. 17 hours since last feed. No pump on board. Send assistance.'

I put everything back on. Initially it is agonising but I try to tune out the pain. I eat three Bourbon creams in the galley on my way upstairs, stuffing them into my mouth one after another, while no one can see.

I wipe the crumbs from my face and grit my teeth as I climb the ladder into the bridge and head back out on deck.

The Department of Environment, Food and Agriculture's fisheries protection vessel *Barrule* in Ramsey Bay with North Barrule in the background.

9

A Future for Our Seas

'Climate change has caused substantial damages, and increasingly irreversible losses, in terrestrial, freshwater and coastal and open ocean marine ecosystems.'

IPCC Summary for Policymakers, 2022

I am on the deck of a fishing boat in the south of Ramsey Bay. I am well wrapped up – under my yellow oilskins I have layers of woollens and thermals. My hat is firmly pushed down on my head, keeping me warm and keeping my hair out of the slimy, sea-tangled mess on the deck and on my hands. We are a mile or so offshore, within the Fisheries Management Zone of the Marine Nature Reserve. I'm working with a couple of the fishermen to count and measure scallops. When we started this work, we'd do this research on the fisheries protection vessel *Barrule* and then feed the results back to the fishermen. Now, the fishermen carry out the surveys themselves and we (government and Bangor University scientists) help out where needed. The fishermen are using specially designed digital measuring boards that send the data back to a computer, avoiding the long process we previously had of measuring each scallop and writing the details down on a slime-smeared waterproof slate or grubby sheet of waterproof paper. It is progress in so many ways and is really helping to put science into the hands of the fishermen. The collection of key scallop biological data – the size of the scallops in the population and the numbers in each size category – can be collected with a small fraction of the effort previously required and there is no 'black box' approach where someone else collects and analyses the data. It is all in their hands.

The fishermen treat it like any other fishing day. The tows have to be made in the agreed areas of the Fisheries Management Zone and the co-ordinates recorded. There is the wait between tows and then the rush as the clanging dredges are hauled aboard and shaken empty one by one onto the deck. Big pale-orange common starfish get wedged in the belly-rings of the dredges and have to be pushed through, and the other by-catch – the clammy stumps of dead men's finger soft corals, another more delicate seven-armed starfish, some sponge and barnacle-encrusted queenies – litters the deck. There isn't really much need for scientists on board now, but scientists and fishermen are particularly interested in seeing the catch first-hand, particularly if the survey is of a site that hasn't been fished for a few years. The excitement of seeing a dredge disgorge its contents of big scallops is immense – in a little-fished area they can be big as dinner plates and up to ten years old, which means they will have been able to reproduce seven or more times before they are caught, boosting populations over a wide area.

Like trees they display their age in rings, most visible on the flat shell, rather than the curved shell. For the skippers and the crew though, this is a first-hand opportunity to gauge how the ground feels and to see for themselves not only the number and size of the scallops but also what else comes up, how much kelp, how many brittlestars and what other clues the dredges can reveal about the seabed. This has been a really important lesson – fishermen will trust science done by fishermen infinitely more than the same studies done by scientists from another vessel.

Having never really intended to breast feed Dylan for as long as I had, as he was approaching two I decided now was the time to wean him. Working full-time, I just tended to feed him in the morning before I left for work and he was looked after by either my parents or our wonderful friend Wensley, and then it was the first thing we did when I picked him up from my parents or I got home, the handover chat accompanied by Dylan enthusiastically suckling. While I'd been lucky enough to travel for work a few times with Dylan and Rob in tow, because of feeding him I hadn't actually left the Island alone since a work trip to Northern Ireland a few months before Dylan was born. I was planning to go to the Channel Islands' Inter-Island Environment Meeting in Alderney at the beginning of October, a month and a half after Dylan turned two, so I decided to use that as my opportunity to wean. I had been to Alderney just before I got pregnant with Dylan and was really looking forward to returning. An island so much smaller than the Isle of Man and with only around 2000 inhabitants, Alderney is wild and quirky and I'd loved it the first time I'd visited to give a presentation about our marine conservation work in the Isle of Man. The first time I went I'd tried to avoid flying to keep my carbon footprint down. I went by ferry and train to Poole and then onwards to Guernsey and then to Alderney, which took nearly two days each way. As this was the first time I'd left Dylan, this time I relented and flew all the way there and back. I was still going to be away for a few days and had mixed feelings about balancing the opportunity to escape and regain my independence with my climate impact and leaving my little family behind.

The trip was a success and the weaning went to plan. In the weeks after Dylan turned two I tried to cut down on feeding times and especially on any feeding at night. By the time I got on the plane to Alderney we were down to a couple of brief feeds a day and we had missed some of those. This preparation wasn't just for Dylan, but also for me. If I'd travelled without reducing the amount I was feeding him, the first few days away could have been really uncomfortable (I still had the memory of that fateful trip on the *Barrule* fresh in my memory!). As it was, it was all relatively painless and when I got back, with some artful distraction and the substitution of a beaker of milk we moved to fully weaned. Shortly after weaning I found that I was pregnant. We'd wanted a second child but the combination of the general pressures of returning to work full-time and the trauma we experienced with the illness and death of Rob's mum in the first two years after Dylan's birth had given us other things to focus on. When we found out I was pregnant, aged nearly forty-three, we were delighted. It felt like a little miracle, and it was. We did the usual thing and decided not to tell anyone until I was twelve weeks. I was a bit concerned because I did a digital test which seemed to show me less pregnant than I calculated I should have been. I went to the doctor and he said not to worry about it but on 5 November, a bonfire night that will always be etched in my memory, I noticed I was bleeding while I was at work.

I went back to my desk and finished whatever I was working on that day, and left work as usual, flying out just in time to get Dylan from nursery before it closed at six o'clock. It usually took a little time to extract Dylan from the train track or the little people (Dylan loved little people; he would arrange dozens of them in queues or crowds or neat rows of audiences – he still does something similar with his more sophisticated Lego minifigures) but, thanks to fate and stars becoming misaligned, on that day, as early fireworks popped in the distance and I walked across the dark car park to the yellow light of the nursery, a mum I didn't know was showing off her days-old baby to the children. Smiling and trying to do a little coo or aah as appropriate (a challenge for me at the best of times), I extricated Dylan from the crowd of adoring toddlers around the newborn babe (it was a cross between a nativity and one of Dylan's little-people scenes), whipped the Velcro open on his slippers and slung them into that smelly box where they all went at the end of the day, got his coat on and bundled him into the car.

We talked on the ten-minute drive from Sulby to Ramsey. I tried to concentrate on Dylan's observations about his day. Even at two he could tell immediately if I wasn't giving him his full attention. 'That's not your normal voice,' he'd say if I answered absently, if I wasn't listening. That would always pull me up.

When I got home I checked again and I was still bleeding but we ate a quick bonfire tea – Rob had made baked potatoes – and walked up Bowring Road to watch fireworks from the brooghs up above the Mooragh park, from where you can see reflections on the lake and in the sea. Some loud music started before the fireworks and that was enough to terrify Dylan and we trooped back down the hill, Dylan on Rob's shoulders, passing happy families still on their way up to find a good viewing spot.

At some point during the evening I was getting something out of a bag on a kitchen chair and Rob was washing something in the sink and Dylan was probably watching *Postman Pat* and I said to Rob 'I think I'm miscarrying' and we just carried on. And later I must have sat on the same dining room chair with the threadbare Victorian seat for quite a long time because afterwards a bloodstain the size of a 2p coin appeared and I left it there to fade over months, as a little private memorial.

In the night Dylan must have got into bed with us, because when I went to the loo, I had to bring a sleepy Dylan with me. I sat him on the step that goes down from the bathroom, facing out onto the dark landing and talking to him as I changed the blood-soaked towel and fleetingly thought that the particularly big glob of blood might actually be the foetus and I wrapped it in toilet tissue and put it in the bin rather than down the loo, just in case.

The next morning I told Rob I was going to A&E and drove over the mountain road in torrential rain at seven a.m.

I saw one of those unbelievably youthful-looking A&E doctors who was very reassuring and told me she was sure it would be fine but she could book me into the early-pregnancy unit to get checked out just in case. I already knew then, but I didn't dispute her smiley optimism. I had to wait for four hours, choosing a small corner with a sofa and a drinks machine which turned out to be right by the stairs down from the maternity ward. The sonographer confirmed what I knew and gave me a hug. I told her it was OK – I had a little boy at home. I felt like I was reassuring her but I also appreciated more than ever just how lucky I was to have him.

I drove back over the mountain road; the rain had eased a little and there were just thick banks of mist to contend with. It's what we think of as Manannán's cloak, thrown over the Island by the Celtic sea god when he is displeased. Wensley had picked Dylan up from nursey at lunchtime and was looking after him at home, so I drove to my parents' house. My mum knew that there was something wrong as soon as she saw me, but she was palpably relieved when she realised it wasn't Dylan. Nothing had happened to Dylan. I slept at my parents' house for the rest of the day and didn't go home until it was normal going-home time, so that I wouldn't have to tell Wensley while it was all still so raw.

And that was it. The faint blood stain reminded me – Rob didn't even notice it until I mentioned that it had completely disappeared. Dylan started calling a rag doll he'd previously not been interested in Sister, which unsettled me.

*

It's my first week back at work following my miscarriage, and I've been called out to a stranded minke whale. I park at Glen Wyllin and walk north. I can just make out the bulk of the creature under the crumbling sandy cliffs that run for much of the coast from Peel to Ballaugh. It is good to be out of the office, but the wind is relentless. The sand is streaming down the beach and I have to pull my hood right down over my eyes as I walk. I can taste the salt and feel the grit on my lips.

I'm not looking forward to this. As a young biologist I was unfazed by death and gore, but this has changed over time. I've become more vulnerable to squeamishness and anthropomorphism. To empathy.

The carcass rises out of the sand, vast and rounded and curiously rosy. The skin is a map of dark patches on a background of bruised white. The tiny minke dorsal fin is folded neatly like a napkin. I secure my backpack under a large stone and measure the creature head to tail, the tape flapping about. Seven metres long – an adult. I need to know its sex, but its underside is already decomposing, and it is impossible to make out the genital opening or the mammary slits.

I am looking for clues to the cause of death. Stranded minke whales often show evidence of tangling. Some are found with rope or cable still attached, others with distinctive marks revealing how they've become bound and drowned. Ship-strikes are surprisingly common too, so any obvious damage to the whale's body also needs to be recorded.

The jaw looks broken, but damage to the extremities of a marine mammal can often happen post-mortem, as they are dashed against the rocky shore. The one visible eye is closed: swollen and mammalian. The sand has scoured a little hollow in the lee of the wind, and fine drifts form under its belly.

I stand on the beach, sand glittering my boots and lodging in my camera. There is a mist of sea and sand; rain threatens from Ireland to the west. I feel so tired. As I look down the beach I don't know if I'll have the energy to walk back against the wind but I start the trudge back to the car.

For around a year after my miscarriage I felt a bit unhinged. I tried everything to get pregnant again (although we didn't go down the IVF route) – a super-healthy diet filled with leafy greens and seeds and chickpeas, a ban on alcohol and regular acupuncture which I discovered I loved. I spent a fortune on specially formulated vitamins and other supplements. I had consultations with local specialists and went to see a fertility expert in London. This was all in the background of a still-busy job, working to take the next steps with our Marine Nature Reserves, considering the future impacts and opportunities of renewable energy developments on our marine environment, and continuing to push forward marine conservation at every opportunity. But all these years later, I still get upset when I see the mum of the newborn baby from the tableau bathed in fluorescent light and smelling faintly of nappies and toddlers' slippers, with her two children. Curiously it is the one thing that never fails to remind me of our loss. A good friend who had her son at the same as I had Dylan got pregnant shortly afterwards and has a daughter who is just a few months younger than that second baby would have been if I hadn't miscarried. But somehow that has never had the impact of that little-known mum and her tiny baby that I saw when I was in the process of realising that I was losing mine.

On my forty-fourth birthday in February 2017, fourteen months after miscarrying, I ceremoniously let go of my longing for that baby we lost. I was on a writing course at Lumb Bank in Heptonstall, West Yorkshire. Lumb Bank and the surrounding countryside is one of my favourite places in the UK. The course coincided with my birthday and also with the Celtic festival of Imbolc that marks the beginning of spring.

In the Isle of Man Imbolc is known as St Brigid's Day or Laa'l Breeshey. Like many ancient Celtic festivals, it has evolved into a curious mix of pagan and Christian tradition but St Brigid, while well known as an Irish saint, is also much commemorated in the Isle of Man. Breeshey or Breesha (along with Voirrey, the Manx for Mary) is one of the best-known Manx Gaelic girls' names. St Brigid reputedly travelled from Ireland to the Isle of Man to receive the veil (and become a nun) from St Maughold, and subsequently founded a nunnery on a site just outside Douglas which is still known as The Nunnery today.

There is a well-known Manx folk song, collected by writer and folklorist Mona Douglas, called 'Vreeshey, Vreeshey' (the 'v' replaced the 'b' following the Manx grammatical convention of mutation or changing the first word of nouns depending on their position in the sentence, a convention in other Celtic languages as well).

A village north of Ramsey is called Bride or Breeshey in Manx and was named after St Brigid. The Manx tradition for Laa'l Breeshey that I had been vaguely aware of was of sweeping the threshold of your house with reeds and inviting St Brigid to visit.

In West Yorkshire that year I participated in the ancient Imbolc ritual of casting away the winter (and with it whatever else we wanted to cast away) and looking forward to spring. We all brought a twig and threw it into the fire and named what we were casting away. What I had articulated in my mind to cast away was the hope for another pregnancy and a child, which at my age seemed vanishingly unlikely, but what came out was the desire to cast away grief and I suppose that summed it up well – grief for the baby that was lost and the lost hope for another.

It may have taken a pagan ritual in the depths of West Yorkshire for me to name my grief, but it was certainly the coast and sea of the Isle of Man that saw me through it (and continues to). I have at various times of my life lived far from the sea and during my journey through the grief of miscarriage and, more recently, in living through the global pandemic, I have never been more grateful for living by the sea. While the pain of that lost pregnancy increased my empathy and sensitivity to the suffering of others, human and animal, and made that call-out to the dead minke whale so soon after my loss particularly painful, the proximity of nature, and the choice to spend time on the shore or in the glens on my own or with my family, has been of immeasurable value.

★

Perhaps the most important legacy that Ramsey MNR left was to pave the way for more Marine Nature Reserves. In 2015 my colleague Peter, who had covered my role during my maternity leave, came back to work with me on a project to expand on what had been achieved in Ramsey Bay and create a full network of MNRs. There was a lot going on in marine conservation, including working with colleagues on new legislation to improve the consenting process for offshore developments, and specifically working on understanding the environmental impact requirements for a proposed offshore windfarm to the east of the Isle of Man.

But proactive marine conservation, like the setting up of new Marine Nature Reserves, remained a priority. Peter led on those next steps forward with MNRs, so we were able to build on the first phase of the Manx Marine Nature Reserve project and expand from one large protected area to the network which I had always hoped for.

So much work over decades informed the progress we'd been able to make with the MNRs. What started with the tiny experimental area in Port Erin and the failed attempt to designate the Calf of Man had been demonstrated to be possible on a much larger scale within Ramsey Marine Nature Reserve. Without the model of a reserve that protected nature and acknowledged the impact and importance of fishing, I don't think it would have been possible to move on to designating 52 per cent of our inshore waters, banning dredging and trawling and offering additional protection.

Peter was originally a scallop scientist and had worked a lot with the fishing industry in previous jobs. He spent a lot of time with the key fishing industry leaders to develop the zoning plan. We worked together to build on the research we'd done for the initial MNR project and developed detailed specification of the features to be protected in the new areas. Once an outline plan was in place, we worked together to consult on the plan, holding drop-in sessions at venues around the Island.

There were some key sticking points with negotiating the network. One of them was around the Calf of Man. As I mentioned at the beginning, this is where it all started with marine conservation in the Isle of Man and the dream of protecting our marine life with a Marine Nature Reserve. The marine life is spectacular, but it has also traditionally been important for scallop dredging so negotiating the boundaries of the new Marine Nature Reserve and banning dredging and trawling within them was particularly challenging. The Calf is close to another conservation hotspot, the less-attractively named Wart Bank. Wart Bank is a big sand bank about five kilometres off the south of the Island. It is a haven for spawning cod and the all-important sand eels that feed so many species of birds and marine mammals like porpoise.

To a scientist, someone plotting out biodiversity hotspots on computer mapping systems and maybe using models and algorithms to highlight where they should be protected, it would seem easy to draw a bigger box around the Calf of Man that would protect the whole area out to the east of the Wart Bank. But it is often these sticking points that risk undermining a whole process. We do need to effectively protect our marine areas, but an element of compromise has worked in the Isle of Man and it is possible for both conservation and fishing to benefit from good management. The area that is now protected was unthinkable in 2004 when I sat in that marine conservation meeting astonished by the concern and what I saw then as lack of ambition and resolve over marine protected areas (but now understand in the context of what had happened not so long before).

Looking out from the Calf of Man over the
Marine Nature Reserve.

This doesn't mean that there isn't a huge amount of work still to be done. In recent years I've gained experience in wider biodiversity and ecosystem management and most recently the Island's response to climate change. But my passion is still the sea. Those now leading this work are continuing the engagement with stakeholders and building the science to improve management of the areas and also ensuring that blue carbon stores are protected. Within the new Marine Nature Reserves are eelgrass beds and horse mussel reefs which could benefit from more bespoke management. While the king and queen scallop fisheries are now very carefully managed, informed by good science, less is understood about the levels of pot-fishing around the Island and the Bangor University scientists are increasingly studying the biology of species like brown crab, lobster and whelk which are among the top commercial fisheries species in the Isle of Man.

Recent evidence from local divers and surveys carried out by DEFA indicates that the eelgrass meadows are spreading and successfully colonising new areas of the Bay. This is great news for climate change, and for the biodiversity of the bay, providing more homes for wonderful charismatic fish like fifteen-spined sticklebacks (which look to me as if they are always smiling) and pipefish. We have at least two species of pipefish: the delicate, almost wire-like snake pipefish, with a flicker of red and white on its head, the only bright colour on an otherwise seagrass-coloured body. The greater pipefish has a much more flattened body and a more recognisably seahorse-like head. Pipefish fascinate me; they are close relatives to seahorses and in my opinion are not appreciated enough. They are tough – they have scaly, almost armour-plated bodies. They are perhaps best known in the UK for choking puffins, which hasn't been great for their reputation. They are prone to population booms where they become super-abundant and paired with the decline in the preferred diet of puffins – lovely, oily, soft-bodied sand eels – are then taken by puffins and because of their tough, armoured body they stick in their throats and kill them. If you search for photos of British pipefish, you will often see images of them peeping coyly out of seagrass, and in my limited experience of them they do seem to do this. They hide out among the stems and keep an eye on things.

What is wonderful about the successful recovery of the eelgrass beds is that it really captured the Island's imagination. The chief minister at the time started mentioning it in speeches, and other politicians got excited about the role of eelgrass in natural carbon capture. I couldn't have been more delighted. And when, in early 2020, a time capsule was put together to bury under the new Isle of Man ferry terminal being built on the banks of the Mersey, I found a clump of eelgrass on the beach at Port Lewaigue after a storm to preserve in alcohol and add to the time capsule, capturing our *zeitgeist*, pre-Covid, of an increased interest in climate action and renewed commitment to the protection of our natural environment.

I'm running on the beach with Dylan. We have both spotted a big strand of kelp and we're racing to get to it first. On both sides of us the bay sweeps in a wide sandy curve, up to the lighthouse at the Point of Ayre in the north and round to Gob ny Rona out to the west. We've played this often – whoever wins the race will wield the kelp like a swooping spell of sea. Embedded in the sand are the bone-white fragments of scallop shell, flat and curved from the perfectly designed bivalve.

Occasionally a darker shell is revealed from under the wind-scoured grains: horse mussels, my beloved gregarious molluscs that clump together to form spectacular reefs, teeming with life out in the deeper channels to the north of the bay. These reefs are nursery grounds for baby whelks and harbour queen scallops, sponges and catshark eggs, and I think of them industriously filtering the waters of the bay and keeping it clean.

Dylan stops in his tracks and snatches something from the sand in front of him. 'Maerl!' he exclaims triumphantly as he shows me the branched coral-like nodules and then stows it quickly in the pocket of his waterproof coat. The maerl beds, pink as cherry blossom, are just a few hundred metres from where we are running, bathed in sunlight and photosynthesising. Living in these beds, I know, are over 300 species of animals. They are a haven for juvenile cod, and the favoured settlement ground for baby queen scallops. The nodules form a criss-cross matrix perfect for hiding tiny creatures.

I reach the kelp first and shriek as I peel it off the beach and hold it aloft like a brown crepe flag. A fine shower of sand scatters in the sunlight.

Dylan screams with delight and runs for the sea, his wellied feet barely indenting the hard sand.

'I'm Manannan! I'm the king of the sea! I'm going to sweep you into my kingdom!' We're both laughing crazily. Dylan has reached the water's edge and has found a floating frond of kelp and he's whirling it around and spraying us both with glimmering droplets of sea. This is pure joy. I take a mental snapshot, better than any I ever remember to take on my phone, then never get round to printing out or saving somewhere sensible. We are two colourful figures on an expanse of tide-scoured sand, dodging and laughing, our feet on the earth, the rising tide swirling a tentative sheet of water around us. Behind us rises the town of Ramsey, a mishmash of old and new, one half demolished and rebuilt in the 1960s, the other half perched on what was previously sand dunes and wetlands. The town is nestled in the ambivalent shadow of North Barrule, with the incongruous neatness of Albert Tower, built to commemorate the visit of Queen Victoria and Prince Albert in 1847 when the Prince Consort was taken to the top of Lhergy Frissel.

On one side the 200-year-old solid bulk of the stone pier each side of the harbour entrance and to the south, the Queen's Pier, a once decaying Victorian structure which a band of enthusiastic volunteers is working hard to restore. The bay has become a symbol of what can be achieved when communities are mobilised, and when environmentalists and fishermen work together. When I look out to sea now, I know that approximately half of the area of the bay is permanently protected from trawling and dredging, and the other half is well managed in the Fisheries Management Zone, with just a small part of that area being fished only once a year in a carefully controlled, science-based fishery. I'm so pleased that the fishermen can now take the lead on this.

When I look out into the bay, I'm now always reminded that within the Marine Nature Reserve, the eelgrass meadows are thriving and spreading out into previously fished areas, to everyone's benefit. After being seconded to work on a climate action plan for the Isle of Man,

I was delighted when the launch of the new plan was covered by the regional BBC news programme with a focus on the role of blue carbon and eelgrass in our fight against climate change. The reporter stood on the shore of Ramsey Marine Nature Reserve, and they showed clips of beautiful emerald eelgrass on the teatime news. We're getting there.

However, another potential threat looms on the horizon. As I write, a company is publicising their plans to infill an area of the beach just south of the stone piers within the Marine Nature Reserve and create a marina, housing and hotels which they claim will boost the local economy and bring wider benefits to Ramsey. But this project could lead to the loss of an area of sand habitat and could impact on some of the eelgrass around the Queen's Pier discovered by scientists in 2019. A development on this scale could also significantly affect the movement of water within the bay, threatening eelgrass meadows and other habitats much more widely. So, at the same time that our eelgrass meadows and marine environment more generally are increasingly being recognised for their wider value, including the important role they could play in mitigating climate change, they are still at risk of damage and destruction in the name of economic development.

For the moment those bright green blades of grass are continuing to spread their roots into new areas of Ramsey Bay and create more shelter and food for hosts of fish and invertebrates. And the rich sandy mud between their roots is locking down carbon from our ailing atmosphere. It is doing its job as part of that hard-working life-support system that surrounds us – our vast blue ocean.

*

It is June 2020 and we've not long emerged from our first lockdown, Dylan is back at school, I'm still working from home most of the time and the weather is glorious. We are allowed to meet with friends and family, although the borders are still closed, so it is only possible to enter the Island under certain circumstances. One evening we head down to Port-e-Vullen after work for a swim. We run into the water together and all swim straight away – it's that warm. The water feels unnaturally warm, smooth and glassy and is a silver metallic blue I haven't seen for a long time. I look back at the little sand and pebble cove with the stream squeezing its way out to sea between a couple of houses, and the rocky edges of the beach, slick with gutweed where the freshwater runs down the beach and hirsute with bladder wrack and knotted wrack. And as I swim a luxuriant, calm, warm-water breaststroke, I'm reconnected to the wider bay. The eelgrass beds are just tens of metres away, sloping gradually off into kelp and then out into the brittlestar beds and maerl and horse mussels further north.

I feel stronger than ever that I am part of the ecosystem, and every centimetre of my body is in contact not just with the bay, but with the global ocean. I savour this for a few minutes, and let myself sink back into the water and float for a few moments, looking up at the sky. And then I have to zoom back into what's going on, because Dylan is out of the water and running up the beach to try to attract the attention of his friend who lives just above.

I love swimming in the sea. I'm back to my eight-year-old self – a sea creature. But on days like today when the water is warmer than I ever remember it being here, I swim in a maelstrom of emotion. I delight in the feeling of the soft clear water around my legs and my body and in the absence of chill. I lick the salty water from my lips. But I know what it means and that breaks my heart.

The Manx sea temperature dataset shows how the average sea temperature around the Isle of Man has increased by around 1°C over the past hundred years. The warmest our waters get is around 16°C towards the end of August, after the summer's heat has been absorbed and accumulates. The sea is coldest in February and March when temperatures hover around 7 to 8°C. This dataset has not only informed decades of marine research in the Isle of Man, from determining what temperature queen scallops become more active and therefore easier to catch, through to predicting when the year's first basking shark might be spotted feeding on plankton in the early summer, but it has also formed part of the global dataset that has provided the evidence for sea temperature increases resulting from global climate change.

For those of us in the British Isles, a continued increase in sea temperatures may seem appealing but the implications are manifold. There are some straightforward consequences of warmer sea. Cool-water species will inevitably move north, following the average sea temperatures to which they are adapted. So, we will see marine animals at the southern end of their range disappearing from our waters. Horse mussels are one such creature and the diversity of their reefs may disappear completely from the Irish Sea within the next couple of decades and could be lost completely from the British Isles well before the end of this century, according to modelling studies carried out by scientists at Heriot-Watt University in Scotland. Warmer-water species and habitats are also expected to become more prevalent, and warmer waters might also benefit non-native invasive species, like the Pacific oyster which is currently found in small numbers in Ramsey Bay, and allow them to outcompete local species that could be lost.

But, as with anything in ecology, it isn't that simple and the truth is that no one can really predict what the impact of increasing sea temperatures will be. Our ecosystems are complex and the seasonality of breeding and spawning, the timing of plankton blooms and growth spurts of seaweed, all have to be carefully synchronised. Changes to spawning timing has already been recorded for sole and cod in the Irish Sea and this really matters. If you are a little planktonic cod floating around on currents, nourished by an egg sac, you are reliant on there being the right kind of planktonic food available for you to move on to when that egg sac runs out. If that plankton hasn't changed its timing too, then you are stuck. Temperature plays a really important role in triggering spawning and enhancing productivity of marine plants and it really matters if the sea temperature is higher than usual in spring or doesn't cool down as quickly in the autumn. The results can be catastrophic.

And there is the added complication of ocean acidification. As concentrations of carbon dioxide have increased in the atmosphere, the ocean has played an important part in absorbing some of that carbon dioxide and helping to reduce the impact on climate. But as the ocean has absorbed around a third of the carbon dioxide released it has become more acidic. It is now estimated that the ocean is 30 per cent more acidic now than at the start of the Industrial Revolution around 200 years ago.

Many sea creatures, from microscopic plankton to coral reefs that fringe whole countries, have a calcium carbonate structure that will be impacted by more acidic waters. Critically, the changes in ocean chemistry will make it more difficult for them to lay down their skeletons in the first place, leading to weaker structures that throughout their lifetime will also be more susceptible to dissolving. Some places around the world are already seeing significant impacts of ocean acidification and it is a global concern.

Epilogue

It is July 2021 and we're in the midst of a heatwave. Rob has recently bought a paddleboard and he's pumping it up in the car park at Port Lewaigue while Dylan and I run into the sea. We barely flinch as we wade in, a combination of water that is warmer than usual and that resilience to chill that comes from regular swimming in the sea. We've swum in the sea at every opportunity this year, and in the colder waters of the Cornaa salmon pool. We've got into the routine of always wearing our swimming things under our clothes when we go for a walk and it has paid off in spontaneous, life-affirming dips. We are in the Eelgrass Zone of Ramsey Bay Marine Nature Reserve, and we watch our step as we wade out, avoiding the little clumps of lettuce-green eelgrass emerging from the sand. Dylan has got his swimming goggles on, and I've brought my mask and snorkel and as soon as it is deep enough we plunge below the surface and start to watch. Dylan spots a little flatfish, a juvenile plaice perfectly camouflaged on the sand until it flits away from us. A school of sand eels whirls ahead of us and disappears and then I see a little shape speed suddenly forwards then plunge down into the sand, leaving just a pair of eyes visible. We hover above the disturbance on the seabed, and then it emerges again and scuds off. It is a little cuttlefish, a tiny cephalopod that will never get any bigger than my thumb. As we swim, we continue to see this tiny predator making a dash for it and then shelter in the sand to watch and wait before emerging again. We've never seen them here before and we exchange wide-eyed be-goggled smiles but daren't put our heads up to speak in case we frighten them away. Sand gobies freeze on the seabed as we pass and only become visible again as they dart away.

Everything is moving. Even though we're trying to drift not flap, we're creating a panic as we float above them, a big shape and a small one. Dylan's hand is on my arm, pointing in excitement as each new thing appears. We examine the little strands of seagrass and swirling stipes of sugar kelp attached to the odd rock here and there.

We're swimming towards The Carrick, the little rocky islet that sits just off Port Lewaigue and is topped by a rusty steel pole with a cylindrical metal cage at the top. The rock is completely submerged at high tide and the pole provides a marker for mariners so that boats can't run aground. We've nearly reached it as Rob paddles over and we haul ourselves onto the paddleboard. Dylan lies on the front and looks down through the water and I sit cross-legged on the back, trying not to move and capsize the family. Rob stands in the middle and paddles slowly and calmly. The surface of the sea is smooth as oarweed and the water is completely clear. Up on the paddleboard we can see the fish on the sandy bottom and as we approach The Carrick, the thickening forest of oarweed kelp appears beneath us. Rob takes the board out around the rock and it looks much bigger close up, speckled all over with bright white barnacles. A cormorant stands like a Liver Bird on top of the metal cage and stretches out its wings to dry. We head into a little inlet among the rocks and climb up onto the tiny island, carefully placing our feet in the shiny salad of seaweed in the shallows and hauling ourselves onto dry land. Dylan is beside himself with excitement, clambering around his little kingdom, calling us over to see the rockpools and limpets and the landscape in miniature of hills and valleys. The rock is warm and the barnacles are small and smooth. We look towards the green wooded slopes of Lewaigue and then north up the Marine Nature Reserve towards the Queen's Pier and beyond.

It is ten years since the Reserve was designated. It has protected the eelgrass and we've seen it spread and thrive and its value in storing away carbon and helping us tackle climate change is now widely known. The horse mussel reefs have been kept safe from the growing whelk fishery which might otherwise have impacted on its fragile structure. I've moved into a new role, working on climate change, and we've just published a consultation on developing the Island's first legally binding climate action plan. On the front cover a seagrass meadow glows green with hope and the potential for a better future.

If we look south, we can see the much bigger islet of Stack Mooar, below Maughold Brooghs. When Dylan was three, in that uncanny way that small children sometimes have, he renamed Stack Mooar in the south of the bay where the eelgrass grows 'Dylanland'. He says it's where he lived before he was born and it is a utopia, where there's no plastic, no pollution, no climate change, no Brexit and, now, no Covid-19 (an eight-year-old who listens to more

Radio 4 than is good for him). Everything is made from natural materials and everything is recycled, and there is a big screen where the children can look into our world and choose the parents they want to live with when they are born. He has spent hours telling us about life in Dylanland. For five years Dylan has filled notebooks with pictures and stories from everyday life there. Somehow, over the past few years Dylanland has become more and more real to me. It sounds like a very nice place to live. We talk about how one day we'll paddleboard further down the coast and land on Dylanland. But in the meantime, we will try to bring a bit more Dylanland to our own lives.

Stack Mooar at low tide.

We clamber back down over the limpets and slide down into the cool arms of the oarweed and we push off back into the water. Rob paddles alongside as Dylan and I swim. We're well out of our depth but Dylan is a strong swimmer and the nearby paddleboard provides a comfort. I catch something large and dark moving in my peripheral vision. I circle back and it is a spider crab, its body the size of a watermelon and long folded legs beneath it. I call to Dylan and Rob and we watch it scuttle. It is gnarled and knobbled and covered in a fur of algae. I dive down to look more closely and Dylan tells me off for scaring it but I tell him it's safe and happy. It's in the most highly protected zone of the Marine Nature Reserve and can't be fished for, if anyone did want this funny creature.

We bob around looking back to shore. This is the warmest July on record for the Isle of Man, which just for this moment I try to put to the back of my mind. It is the last week of term and the beach is full of families who have come down straight after school – I've never seen it so busy. Through the winter and spring this is a beach that Dylan and I had got used to having to ourselves on our morning low-tide walks through the second and third lockdowns. But it is wonderful to see so many people enjoying this little corner of the Marine Nature Reserve. There is an older couple swimming just offshore who look like they might be on holiday, and others who seem to be regulars to the beach stride down and dive in. Young women share kayaks and paddle north towards the Queen's Pier. One man tries out his new snorkelling kit – the type with the full-face mask and integrated snorkel like a trunk at the top – submerging then popping back up to adjust the strap or wipe condensation from the inside. A young couple expertly paddleboard past, looking like they might be covering quite a distance. And surveying the scene from the sea, just out of my depth and with eelgrass and cuttlefish and spider crabs beneath me, I realise that this is the vision that I had in 2008 and which was captured in so many of those yellow sticky notes on the board in the Villa Marina foyer at that first workshop. The marine life is thriving and people are finally using the Marine Nature Reserve and appreciating having such beauty and wonder on their own doorsteps. The Marine Nature Reserve, the science and surveys, the negotiations and compromises, the colourful information boards and all the efforts made over the years to let people know about it – all this has made a difference. But it has taken a global pandemic and closed borders to make us really appreciate what we have. I do hope that this shift in focus to our local environment and people's newfound enthusiasm for doing the things that many of us only usually do on holiday somewhere else – kayaking, paddleboarding, swimming in the sea – right here on our wonderful doorstep, will continue. It can only be a good thing; more people connecting to the sea and, enveloped in it or floating on it, beginning to understand its power and its importance.

As I write this, I'm increasingly encouraged with the way that marine conservation and in particular restoration and rewilding are now being embraced, around the British Isles and across the world. I was recently able to join online the first big international conservation congress since the beginning of the pandemic, the IUCN Congress in Marseille, and there was so much encouraging talk of putting nature at the heart of climate policy and rethinking our relationship with nature completely. In the Isle of Man, the first phase of a new blue carbon project has just been funded which has the scope to take the transformation of our territorial sea and the way we view it a step further. Projects in Wales and Scotland and England are beginning to restore eelgrass and oysters on a scale that was unimaginable just a decade ago.

With the Marine Nature Reserve stretching off to the north and the horizon misty and indistinct, we drift and float and swim slowly back to the shore, calling to each other. I dive down periodically to look more closely at the waving bunches of eelgrass, always hoping that I might see a pipefish, another little cuttlefish or maybe even that first elusive seahorse. Bathed in salt water, with Dylan's beaming face popping up every so often and the pull and drip of Rob paddling nearby, anything seems possible. We can harness the superpowers of the ocean, we can restore our seas, we can change the world.

References and
Further Reading

Prologue and Chapter 1 – Coming Home

Beukers-Stewart B.D., B.J. Vause, M.W.J. Mosley, H.L. Rossetti and A.R. Brand (2005). Benefits of closed area protection for a population of scallops. *Marine Ecology Progress Series* 298: 189–204.

Bowen S., C. Goodwin, D. Kipling and B. Picton (2018). *Sea Squirts and Sponges of Britain and Ireland.* Wild Nature Press.

Bradshaw C., L.O. Veale, A.S. Hill and A.R. Brand (2001). The effect of scallop dredging on Irish Sea benthos: Experiments using a closed area. *Hydrobiologia* 465: 129–138.

Bradshaw C., L.O. Veale, A.S. Hill and A.R. Brand (2002). The role of scallop-dredge disturbance in long-term changes in Irish Sea benthos: Experiments using a closed area. *Hydrobiologia* 465: 129–138.

Bunker F. (2017). *Seaweeds of Britain and Ireland.* Wild Nature Press.

Caine H. (1891). *Little Manx Nation.* William Heinemann.

Chiverrell R., G. Thomas, S. Duffy, H.C. Mytum and

J. Belchem (2000). *A New History of the Isle of Man.* Liverpool University Press.

DAFF (1992). The Calf of Man: A proposed Marine Nature Reserve. Consultation document.

Forbes E. (1838). *Malacologia Monensis: A Catalogue of the Mollusca Inhabiting the Isle of Man and the Neighbouring Sea.* John Carfrae & Son.

Garrad L.S. (1972). *The Naturalist in the Isle of Man.* David & Charles.

Gubbay S. (2000). Review of sites of Marine Nature Conservation Importance around the Isle of Man. A report to the Manx Wildlife Trust.

Hill A.S., L.O. Veale, D. Pennington, S.G. Whyte, A.R. Brand and R.G. Hartnoll (1999). Changes in Irish Sea benthos: Possible effects of forty years of dredging. *Estuarine and Coastal Shelf Science* 48: 739–750.

Jenkins S.R., B. Beukers-Stewart and A.R. Brand (2001). The impact of scallop dredging on benthic megafauna: A comparison of damage levels in captured and non-captured organisms. *Marine Ecology Progress Series* 215: 297–301.

Marshall W.L. (1978). *The Calf of Man.* Shearwater Press.

Picton B.E. and C.C. Morrow (1994). *A Field Guide to the Nudibranchs of the British Isles.* Immel Publishing.

Sanderson B., B. McGregor and A. Brierley (1994). *Dive Sites and Marine Life of the Calf of Man and Neighbouring Area.* Immel Publishing.

Smale D.A., A. Pessarrodona, N. King and P.J. Moore (2021). Examining the production, export, and immediate fate of kelp detritus on open-coast subtidal reefs in the Northeast Atlantic. *Limnology and Oceanography.* doi:10.1002/lno.11970

Chapter 2 – The Sweetest of Bays

Barnes D.K.A., A. Corrie, M. Whittington, C.M. Antonio and F.R. Gell (1998). Coastal shellfish resource use in the Quirimba Archipelago, Mozambique. *Journal of Shellfish Research* 17(1): 51–58.

Forbes E. (1841). *A History of British Starfishes and Other Animals of the Class Echinodermata*. J. Van Voorst.

Forbes E. and S.C.T. Hanley (1853). *A History of British Mollusca and Their Shells*. J. Van Voorst.

Garner R. (1878). Professor Edward Forbes and his country. *Midland Naturalist* 1: 67–70.

Gell F.R. and C.M. Roberts (2003). Benefits beyond boundaries: The fishery effects of marine reserves. *Trends in Ecology & Evolution* 18: 448–455.

Gell F.R. and M.W. Whittington (2002). Diversity of fishes in seagrass beds in the Quirimba Archipelago, northern Mozambique. *Marine and Freshwater Research* 53: 115–121.

Orth R.J., J.S. Lefcheck, K.S. McGlathery, L. Aoki, M.W. Luckenbach, K.A. Moore et al. (2020). Restoration of seagrass habitat leads to rapid recovery of coastal ecosystem services. *Science Advances* 6: eabc6434. doi:10.1126/sciadv.abc6434

Roberts C.M., J.A. Bohnsack, F.R. Gell, J. Hawkins and R. Goodridge (2001). Effects of marine reserves on adjacent fisheries. *Science* 294: 1920–1923.

Roberts C.M., J.P. Hawkins and F.R Gell (2005). The role of marine reserves in achieving sustainable fisheries. *Philosophical Transactions of the Royal Society of London B* 360: 123–132.

Unsworth R.K.F, L.J. McKenzie, C.J. Collier, L.C. Cullen-

Unsworth, C.M. Duarte, J.S. Eklöf et al. (2018). Global challenges for seagrass conservation. *Ambio* 48(8): 801–815.

Chapter 3 – The King of the Sea

Ball B.J., G. Fox and B.W. Munday (2000). Long- and short-term consequences of a *Nephrops* trawl fishery on the benthos and environment of the Irish Sea. *ICES Journal of Marine Science* 57: 1315–1320.

Bergmann M., S.K. Wieczorek, P.G Moore and R.J.A. Atkinson (2002). Discard composition of the *Nephrops* fishery in the Clyde Sea area, Scotland. *Fisheries Research* 57: 169–183. doi:10.1016/S0165-7836(01)00345-9.

Brander K. (1981). Disappearance of common skate *Raia batis* from Irish Sea. *Nature* 290(5801): 48–49.

Bruce J.R., J.S. Colman and N.S. Jones (1963). *Marine Fauna of the Isle of Man*. Liverpool University Press.

Dickey-Collas M., R.D.M. Nash and J. Brown (2001). The location of spawning of Irish Sea herring (*Clupea harengus*). *Journal of the Marine Biological Association of the UK* 81: 713–714.

Ellis J.R., S. Milligan, L. Readdy, A. South, N. Taylor and M. Brown (2010). Mapping spawning and nursery areas of species to be considered in Marine Protected Areas (Marine Conservation Zones). Report No. 1: Final report on development of derived data layers for 40 mobile species considered to be of conservation importance. Cefas, Lowestoft.

Engelhard G.H., R.H. Thurstan, B.R. MacKenzie, H.K. Alleway, R.C.A. Bannister, M. Cardinale et al. (2016).

ICES meets marine historical ecology: Placing the history of fish and fisheries in current policy context. *ICES Journal of Marine Science* 73(5): 1386–1403.

Fargher D. (1969). *The Manx Have a Word for It – Book 2: Marine Flora and Fauna*. Self-published pamphlet.

Fargher D. (1979). *Fargher's English-Manx Dictionary*. B. Stowell and I. Faulds, eds. Shearwater Press.

Geffen A.J., R.D.M. Nash and M. Dickey-Collas (2011). Characterisation of herring populations west of the British Isles: An investigation of mixing based on otolith biochemistry. *ICES Journal of Marine Science* 68(7): 1447–1458.

Kay P. and F. Dipper (2009). *A Field Guide to the Marine Fishes of Wales and Adjacent Waters*. Marine Wildlife.

Moore A.W. (1924). *A Vocabulary of the Anglo-Manx Dialect*. E. Goodwin and S. Morrison, eds. Oxford University Press.

Morrison S. (1911). *Manx Fairy Tales*. David Nutt.

Roberts C. (2007). *An Unnatural History of the Sea*. Island Press.

Smith W.C. (1923). *A Short History of the Irish Sea Herring Fisheries During the Eighteenth and Nineteenth Centuries*. Special Publications 1, Port Erin Biological Station. University of Liverpool Press and Hodder & Stoughton.

Chapter 4 – Diving In

Barbera C., C. Bordehore, J.A. Borg, M. Glémarec, J. Grall, J.M. Hall-Spencer et al. (2003). Conservation and management of Northeast Atlantic and Mediterranean maerl beds. *Aquatic Conservation: Marine and Freshwater Ecosystems* 13(S1): 65–76.

Butler P.G., C.A. Richardson, J.D. Scourse, A.D. Wanamaker, T.M. Shammon and J.D. Bennell (2010). Marine
climate in the Irish Sea: Analysis of a 489-year marine
master chronology derived from growth increments in
the shell of the clam *Arctica islandica*. *Quaternary Science
Review* 29: 1614–1632.

Butler P.G., A. Wanamaker, J. Scourse, C. Richardson and D.
Reynolds (2013). Variability of marine climate on the
North Icelandic Shelf in a 1357-year proxy archive based
on growth increments in the bivalve *Arctica islandica*.
Palaeogeography, Palaeoclimatology, Palaeoecology 373: 21-30.

Chen I., K. Hartman, M. Simmonds, A. Wittich and A.J.
Wright, eds (2013). *Grampus griseus* 200th anniversary:
Risso's dolphins in the contemporary world. Report
from the European Cetacean Society Conference
Workshop, Galway, Ireland. European Cetacean Society
Special Publication Series No. 54.

Cook R.L, J.M. Fariñas-Franco, F.R. Gell, R.H.F. Holt, T.
Holt, C. Lindenbaum et al. (2013). The substantial first
impact of bottom fishing on rare biodiversity hotspots:
A dilemma for evidence-based conservation. PLOS One
8(8): e69904.

Fariñas-Franco J.M. and D. Roberts (2018). The relevance
of reproduction and recruitment to the conservation
and restoration of keystone marine invertebrates: A case
study of sublittoral *Modiolus modiolus* reefs impacted by
demersal fishing. *Aquatic Conservation* 28(3): 672–689.

Gormley K., J.S. Porter, M.C. Bell, A.D. Hull and W.G.
Sanderson (2013). Predictive habitat modelling as a
tool to assess the change in distribution and extent of
an OSPAR priority habitat under an increased ocean

temperature scenario: Consequences for Marine Protected Area networks and management. *PLOS ONE* 8: e68263. doi:10.1371/journal.pone.006826

Green A.E., R.K.F Unsworth, M.A. Chadwick and P.J.S. Jones (2021). Historical analysis exposes catastrophic seagrass loss for the United Kingdom. *Frontiers in Plant Science* 12: 629962.

Hall-Spencer J.M., J. Grall, P.G. Moore and R.J.A. Atkinson (2003). Bivalve fishing and maerl-bed conservation in France and the UK – retrospect and prospect. *Aquatic Conservation: Marine and Freshwater Ecosystems* 13(S1): S33–S41.

Hextall B. and M. Mitchell (1994). *Dive the Isle of Man.* Underwater World Publications.

Hinz H., L. Murray and M.J. Kaiser (2008). Side-scan-sonar survey of the horse mussel (*Modiolus modiolus*) beds off the Point of Ayre (August 2008). Fisheries & Conservation report no. 4, Bangor University, p. 19.

Hiscock K. (2018). *Exploring Britain's Hidden World: A Natural History of Seabed Habitat.* Wild Nature Press.

Kamenos N.A., P.G. Moore and J.M. Hall-Spencer (2004a). Attachment of the juvenile queen scallop (*Aequipecten opercularis* (L.)) to maerl in mesocosm conditions; juvenile habitat selection. *Journal of Experimental Marine Biology and Ecology* 306: 139–155.

Kamenos N.A., P.G. Moore and J.M. Hall-Spencer (2004b). Maerl grounds provide both refuge and high growth potential for juvenile queen scallops (*Aequipecten opercularis* L.). *Journal of Experimental Marine Biology and Ecology* 313: 241–254.

Kamenos N.A., P.G. Moore and J.M. Hall-Spencer (2004c). Nursery-area function of maerl grounds for juvenile queen scallops *Aequipecten opercularis* and other invertebrates. *Marine Ecology-Progress Series* 274: 183–189.

Kent F.E.A, J.M. Mair, J. Newton, C. Lindenbaum, J.S. Porter and W.G. Sanderson (2017). Commercially important species associated with horse mussel (*Modiolus modiolus*) biogenic reefs: A priority habitat for nature conservation and fisheries benefits. *Marine Pollution Bulletin* 118(1–2): 71–78.

Knight M. and M.W. Parke (1931). *Manx Algae*. Liverpool Marine Biological Committee, Memoir 30. Liverpool University Press.

Laffoley, D and G. Grimsditch eds (2009). The management of natural coastal carbon sinks. IUCN report.

Lovelock C.E., J.W. Fourqurean and J.T. Morris (2017). Modelled CO_2 emissions from coastal wetland transitions to other land uses: Tidal marshes, mangrove forests, and seagrass beds. *Frontiers in Marine Science* 4: 143. doi:10.3389/fmars.2017.00143

Marbà N., A. Arias-Ortiz, P. Masqué, G.A. Kendrick, I. Mazarrasa, G.R. Bastyan et al. (2015). Impact of seagrass loss and subsequent revegetation on carbon sequestration and stocks. *Journal of Ecology* 103: 296–302. doi:10.1111/1365-2745.12370

MCCIP (2018). Climate change and marine conservation: Horse mussel beds. M. Smedley, C. Mackenzie, J. Fariñas-Franco, F. Kent, K. Gilham, L. Kamphausen et al., eds. doi:10.14465.2018.ccmco.002-hom

Naylor P. (2021). *Great British Marine Animals*. Sound Diving Publications.

Porter J. (2012). *Bryozoans and Hydroids of Britain and Ireland.* Wild Nature Press.

Porter J.S., R. Seed, L.R. Skates, T.B. Stringell and W.G. Sanderson (2013). The substantial first impact of bottom fishing on rare biodiversity hotspots: A dilemma for evidence-based conservation. *PLOS One* 8: e69904, doi:10.1371/journal.pone.0069904

Roberts C.M., F.R. Gell and J.P. Hawkins (2003). Protecting nationally important marine areas in the Irish Sea Pilot project region. Report to the Department of the Environment, Food and Rural Affairs, UK.

Selman R.G. and A.J. Cherrill (2018). The lesser mottled grasshopper, *Stenobothrus stigmaticus*: Lessons from habitat management at its only site in the British Isles. *Journal of Orthoptera Research* 27(1): 83–89.

Tauran A., J. Dubreuil, B. Guyonnet and J. Grall (2020). Impact of fishing gears and fishing intensities on maerl beds: An experimental approach. *Journal of Experimental Marine Biology and Ecology* 533: 151472.

United Nations Environment Programme (2020). Out of the blue: The value of seagrasses to the environment and to people. UNEP, Nairobi.

Veale L., R. Thompson and M. Bates (1998). Isle of Man sublittoral survey 1994–1997. Port Erin Marine Laboratory, Isle of Man.

Wood C. (2018). *The Diver's Guide to Marine Life of Britain and Ireland.* Wild Nature Press.

Chapter 5 – Marine Conservation

Caine H. (1923). *The Woman of Knockaloe.* Cassell.

Dialogue Matters (2008). Manx Marine Nature Reserve Stakeholder Workshop. Workshop outputs. DAFF, Isle of Man Government and Dialogue Matters.

Earll B. (2018). *Marine Conservation: People, Ideas, Action.* Pelagic Publishing.

MacLeod C.D., M.B. Santos, R.J Reid, B.E. Scott and G.J. Pierce (2007). Linking sandeel consumption and the likelihood of starvation in harbour porpoises in the Scottish North Sea: Could climate change mean more starving porpoises? *Biology Letters* 3(2): 185–188.

Sharpe C.M., J.P. Bishop, J.P Cullen, P.G. Giovannini, J.P. Thorpe and P. Weaver (2007). *Manx Bird Atlas.* Liverpool University Press.

Chapter 6 – Ocean Giants

Doherty P.D., J.M. Baxter, F.R. Gell, B.J. Godley, R.T. Graham, G. Hall et al. (2017). Long-term satellite tracking reveals variable seasonal migration strategies of basking sharks in the north-east Atlantic. *Scientific Reports* 7: 42837. doi:10.1038/srep42837

Dolton H.R., F.R. Gell, J. Hall, G. Hall, L.A. Hawkes and M.J. Witt (2020). Assessing the importance of Isle of Man waters for the basking shark *Cetorhinus maximus. Endangered Species Research* 41: 209–223. doi:10.3354/esr01018

Gore M.A., D. Rowat, J. Hall, F.R. Gell and R.F. Ormond (2008). Transatlantic migration and deep mid-ocean diving by basking shark. *Biology Letters* 4: 395–398.

Graham N.A.J., S.K Wilson, P. Carr, A.S. Hoey, S. Jennings and M.A. MacNeil (2018). Seabirds enhance coral reef productivity and functioning in the absence of invasive rats. *Nature* 559: 250–253. doi:10.1038/s41586-018-0202-3

Kovalchuk O. and Z. Barkaszi (2021). Oligocene basking sharks (Lamniformes, Cetorhinidae) of the Carpathian Basin with a reconsideration of the role of gill rakers in species diagnostics. *Journal of Vertebrate Paleontology* 41: 2.

Lieber L., G. Hall, J. Hall, S. Berrow, E. Johnston, C. Gubili et al. (2020). Spatio-temporal genetic tagging of a cosmopolitan planktivorous shark provides insight to gene flow, temporal variation and site-specific re-encounters. *Scientific reports* 10(1): 1661.

Parker H.W. and F.C. Stott (1965). Age, size and vertebral calcification in the basking shark, *Cetorhinus maximus* (Gunnerus). *Zoologische Mededelingen* 40: 305–319.

Pinnegar J.K. and M. Heath (2010). Fish in MCCIP annual report card 2010–11. *MCCIP Science Review*, www.mccip.org.uk/arc

Speedie C. (2017). *A Sea Monster's Tale: In Search of the Basking Shark.* Wild Nature Press.

Wallace S. and B. Gisborne (2006). *Basking Sharks: The Slaughter of BC's Gentle Giants.* Transmontanus/New Star Books.

Chapter 7 – Ramsey Bay

Cadman P. and A. Nelson-Smith (1993). A new species of lugworm: *Arenicola defodiens sp. nov. Journal of the Marine Biological Association of the United Kingdom* 73(1): 213–223. doi:10.1017/S0025315400032744

Geffen A., S.J. Hawkins and E.M. Fisher (1990). The Isle of Man in the Irish Sea: An environmental review. Part

1 – nature conservation. Irish Sea Forum and Liverpool University Press.

Gell F.R. and L. Hanley (2010). Developing a Marine Nature Reserve for Ramsey. Full consultation document. Department of Environment, Food and Agriculture, Isle of Man Government.

Hawkins S.J., A.J. Geffen and E.M. Fisher (1990). The status of marine nature conservation in the Isle of Man. A report to the Isle of Man Government. Port Erin Marine Laboratory and University of Liverpool.

Hinz H., L.G. Murray, F.R. Gell, L. Hanley, N. Horton, H. Whiteley et al. (2010). Seabed habitats around the Isle of Man. Fisheries & Conservation report no. 12, Bangor University, p. 29.

Kennington K. (2011). Ramsey Bay Marine Nature Reserve base-line survey (August 2011). Preliminary report. DEFA, Isle of Man.

Koskinen M. (2004). Selecting sites for Marine Protected Areas in Isle of Man coastal waters. MRes placement project report to DAFF.

Pikesley S.K., J.-L. Solandt, C. Trundle and M.J Witt (2021). Benefits beyond 'features': Cooperative monitoring highlights MPA value for enhanced seabed integrity. *Marine Policy* 134: 104801. doi:10.1016/j.marpol.2021.104801

White S. (2011). Biotope distribution and susceptibility to fishing pressure. MSc thesis, Bangor University.

Chapter 8 – Success

Bloor I., P.F Duncan, S. Dignan, J. Emmerson, D. Beard, F.R. Gell et al. (2021). Boom not bust: Cooperative management as a mechanism for improving the commercial efficiency and environmental outcomes of regional scallop fisheries. *Marine Policy* 132: 104649.

Harris M.P., M. Newell, F. Daunt, J.R. Speakman and S. Wanless (2008). Snake pipefish *Entelurus aequoreus* are poor food for seabirds. *Ibis* 150(2): 413–415.

Parker R.W.R., J.L. Blanchard, C. Gardner, B.S. Green, K. Hartmann, P.H. Tyedmers and R.A. Watson (2018). Fuel use and greenhouse gas emissions of world fisheries. *Nature Climate Change* 8: 333–337. doi:10.1038/s41558-018-0117-x

Wood C. (2013). *Sea Anemones and Corals of Britain and Ireland*. Second edition. Wild Nature Press.

Chapter 9 – A Future for Our Seas

Duarte C.M., S. Agusti, E. Barbier, G.L. Britten, J.C. Castilla, J.-P. Gattuso et al. (2020). Rebuilding marine life. *Nature* 580(7801): 39–51. doi:10.1038/s41586-020-2146-7

Earle S.A. (2009). The World Is Blue: How Our Fate and the Ocean's Are One. *National Geographic Society*.

Gattuso J.-P., A.K. Magnan, L. Bopp, W.W.L. Cheung, C.M. Duarte, J. Hinkel et al. (2018). Ocean solutions to address climate change and its effects on marine ecosystems. *Frontiers in Marine Science* 5: 337.

Hoegh-Guldberg O., E. Northrop and J. Lubchenco (2019). The ocean is key to achieving climate and social goals. *Science* 365: 1372–1374.

IPCC (2022). Summary for Policymakers. H.-O. Pörtner, D.C. Roberts, E.S. Poloczanska, K. Mintenbeck, M. Tignor, A. Alegría et al., eds. In: *Climate Change*

2022: Impacts, Adaptation, and Vulnerability. Contribution of Working Group II to the Sixth Assessment Report of the Intergovernmental Panel on Climate Change. Cambridge University Press. In press.

Laffoley D., J.M. Baxter, D.J. Amon, J. Claudet, C.A. Downs, S.A. Earle et al. (2021). The forgotten ocean: Why COP26 must call for vastly greater ambition and urgency to address ocean change. *Aquatic Conservation: Marine and Freshwater Ecosystems* 32(1): 217– 228.

Reynard N., E. Ellison, A. Wilson, P. Williamson, J. O'Niles, E. Ransome et al. (2020). The contribution of coastal blue carbon ecosystems to climate change mitigation and adaptation. Grantham Institute, Imperial College London. doi:10.25561/84458

Roberts C.M., B.C. O'Leary, D.J. McCauley, P.M. Cury, C.M. Duarte, J. Lubchenco et al. (2017). Marine reserves can mitigate and promote adaptation to climate change. *Proceedings of the National Academy of Sciences of the USA* 114: 6167.

Seddon N., A. Chausson, P. Berry, C.A.J. Girardin, A. Smith and B. Turner (2020). Understanding the value and limits of nature-based solutions to climate change and other global challenges. *Philosophical Transactions of the Royal Society B* 375: 20190120.

Worm B., C. Elliff, J.G. Fonseca, F.R. Gell, C. Serra-Gonçalves, N.K. Helder et al. (2021). Making ocean literacy inclusive and accessible. *Ethics in Science and Environmental Politics* 21: 1–9.

Acknowledgements

First, a note and an apology. I originally set out to write about horse mussels not humans, so in telling the people part of the story I am writing about my experience and I must apologise for anything I've misremembered or mis-represented, and also for the many parts of the story that I've not been able to include in this condensed account.

This book has taken a long time and has evolved signif-icantly, and I have so many people to thank (while taking full responsibility for any errors that have crept in).

Thank you to Gaia Banks for venturing all the way to the Isle of Man to Manx LitFest, and for becoming the best possible agent I could imagine. And to my wonderful editor Maddy Price, who took on my sea book and helped me to transform it into a story. Without these two fabulous women this book would never have come into being – thank you! Thanks also to Rosie Pearce and to all at Orion for seeing me through the final stages.

Over the years I've been fortunate enough to do writing courses with some of the most amazing writers. Thanks to Monique Roffey, Helen Scales, Tiffany Murray, Neil Roll-inson, Greta Stoddart, Horatio Clare, Romesh Gunesekera, Kate Pullinger, Charlotte du Cann, Lucy Neal, Jim Crace,

Martha Sprackland and many more for their inspiration and instruction.

Thank you to John Quirk and all those at Manx LitFest for bringing great writers (and agents) to the Isle of Man, and to Isle of Man poets Janet Lees and Usha Kishore for their inspiration and encouragement. And Jonathan Ruppin for his encouragement and advice.

I would like to thank Fiona McCardle at Yn Cheshaght Ghailckagh for her help with seeking permission to use extracts from Douglas Fargher's English–Manx dictionary and finding out more about his life and work. Thanks to Wendy Thirkettle at the Manx National Heritage Library and Archive for providing permission on behalf of Manx National Heritage to use extracts from the works of Mona Douglas. Thanks to Dr Breesha Maddrell of Culture Vannin for advice, support and encouragement. Thanks to Culture Vannin for a grant which supported the development of this book.

I also want to thank all those who have worked tirelessly to study, protect and manage the marine life of the Isle of Man. Thanks to Liz Charter for taking me on as the first marine conservation officer, having the vision for Manx MPAs and for doing so much to protect Manx biodiversity over the years, and to Laura Hanley who worked tirelessly on the Manx Marine Nature Reserve Project. Thanks to my former Isle of Man Government colleagues (past and present) who have worked to protect our most special of seas; Dr Peter Duncan, Rowan Henthorn, Andy Read, Karen McHarg, Dr Kev Kennington, Dr Jack Emmerson, Dr Isobel Bloor, Dr Emma Rowan, Dr Calum MacNeil, Neil Milsom, Joy Eaton, Rob Annett, Rebecca Richardson and all in the DEFA Fisheries team.

Thanks to Richard Lole for supporting my request for a writing sabbatical and to all of the wonderful Ecosystems Policy team – sorry for abandoning you for a year and then defecting to climate change.

Thanks to brilliant Manx marine conservationist Dr Lara Howe and environmental educator Dawn Colley of the Manx Wildlife Trust who have both championed Ramsey Bay Marine Nature Reserve at every opportunity, Jackie and Graham Hall of Manx Basking Shark Watch and Tony Glen who formerly ran Seasearch Isle of Man; Manx Fish Producers' Organisation CEO Dr David Beard and his predecessor Tom Bryan-Brown and all the fishermen of the MFPO for all that they have done to support marine conservation; the amazing former staff and alumni of Port Erin Marine Laboratory; Dr John Thorpe, Dr Andy Brand, Dr Richard Hartnoll, Mike Bates, Dr Terry Holt, Dr Salma Shalla, Dr Jan Gledhill, Prof. Stuart Jenkins, Dr Roger Pullin, Prof. Steve Hawkins, Theresa Shammon, Dr Bryce Stewart, Dr Bob Earll, Dr Ben Hextall, Dr Lewis Veale, Dr Erica Spencer, Dr Ruth Thurstan, Dr Richard Nash and Prof. Audrey Geffen and so many others; divers and discoverers of new habitats Caroline Perry and Phil Roriston, Steve Knowles, Dr Michelle Haywood and Keith McKay. There are so many other scientists whose work has contributed to Manx marine conservation in recent years including Prof. Bill Sanderson, Dr Clara Mackenzie, Dr Jo Porter, Dr José Fariñas-Franco, Bernard Picton, Dr Sue Gubbay, Dr Maija Marsh, Haley Dolton, Dr Rob Cooke, Prof. Michel Kaiser and so many others that I apologise for not mentioning by name. Thanks to Diana Pound for her invaluable stakeholder engagement advice and support.

Thanks also to my marine friends, mentors and collaborators further afield who have inspired and informed me: Dr Jerry Kemp, Prof. Callum Roberts, Dr Julie Hawkins, Dr Liz Ashton, Prof. Rupert Ormond, Prof. Alistair Edwards and Dr Emily Hardman. And in memory of three Manx marine stalwarts who have left us in recent years: Maura Mitchell, Prof. Trevor Norton and William Cain.

Thanks to my friends Wensley Higgins, Vita Martin, Aline Thomas, Vilma Svedkauskiene, Lee Harrison, Jill Dunlop, Alison Clague, Claire Hickson, Diane Kingston, Wendy Dixon, Nicola Makanjuola and Dr Ros Miles for their encouragement and support. Enormous thanks to Louise Beckett who has inspired and encouraged me throughout this process.

Extra special thanks to my parents Dave and Hazel Gell for all their support and encouragement over the years, for being wonderful grandparents and for the opportunity to grow up by the sea surrounded by books. And in memory of Nancy, my Manx Grandma who loved the sea and Maisie, my English Grandma who loved poetry. Thanks to also to Tristan Gell, Ruth Keggin Gell, Cyril Jones and Sian Jones, and in memory of Brenda Jones who loved Manx nature.

And finally, to Rob, who has encouraged and supported me throughout this project and in my work in conservation and climate change, and to Dylan, who has inspired and enthused me and provided a daily reminder of our responsibility to the future of this planet. Thanks to both of you for making me laugh and spurring me on. I couldn't have done this without you.

Text Credits

Extract from the poem 'A Sea-Chantey' from *In a Green Night* by Derek Walcott reprinted with the kind permission of Derek Walcott Estate.

Extracts from *This Is Ellan Vannin Again: Folklore* and *Ellynyn Ny Gael Manx Plays* – 'Teeval of the Sea' by Mona Douglas with the kind permission of Manx National Heritage.

Extracts from *Fargher's English-Manx Dictionary* by Douglas Fargher, Shearwater Press, Isle of Man. This book is out of print and I was not able to trace a copyright holder.

Extract from 'Basking Shark' by Norman MacCaig from *The Poems of Norman MacCaig*, Polygon, reprinted with the kind permission of Birlinn Limited.

Image Credits

All photos are the author's own or family photos with the exception of the below, which have been used with the kind permission of the following people:

p. 51   Callum Roberts
p. 93   Caroline Perry and Phil Roriston
p. 96   Keith McKay
p. 98   Caroline Perry and Phil Roriston
p. 104 Caroline Perry and Phil Roriston
p. 111 Rohan Holt
p. 135 Copyright of The Knockaloe Charitable Trust www.knockaloe.im and reproduced with their permission.
p. 154 Alamy
p 182   Illustration of Ramsey Bay Marine Nature Reserve by John Caley. Reproduced with permission of the Department of Environment, Food and Agriculture.